Communist Politics in Britain

Hugo Dewar

Communist Politics in Britain

The CPGB from its Origins to the Second World War

Pluto Press

First published 1976 by Pluto Press Limited
Unit 10 Spencer Court, 7 Chalcot Road, London NW1 8LH
Copyright © Pluto Press 1976

ISBN 0 904383 04 0

Printed by Bristol Typesetting Company Limited
Barton Manor, St Philips, Bristol

Cover Picture: First Central Committee of the
Communist Party of Great Britain,
James Klugmann Collection
Cover design by Kate Hepburn

Contents

Contents

Acknowledgements

I should like to recall here the names of those old-time members of the Communist Party – now, alas, dead – who provided me with party publications and gave me the benefit of their knowledge and understanding and the pleasure of their good fellowship: Jim Barrett, Stewart Purkis, Henry Sara. I am much indebted to Reg Groves for his kind encouragement and valuable advice. I am profoundly grateful to Harry Wicks, who by his experienced guidance and unstinting aid contributed so much to the completion of this book.

It goes without saying that without the support of my dear friend and companion, Margaret, this small contribution to the cause of socialism could not have been made.

Abbreviations

ARC: Anglo-Russian Committee
AUCCTU: All-Union Central Council of Trade Unions
BSP: British Socialist Party
CC: Central Committee
CI: Communist International, Comintern
CP/CPGB: Communist Party of Great Britain
CPSU: Communist Party of the Soviet Union
ECCI: Executive Committee of the Communist International
IFTU: International Federation of Trade Unions (Amsterdam)
ILP: Independent Labour Party
IWW: Industrial Workers of the World
NMM: National Minority Movement
NUR: National Union of Railwaymen
NUWM: National Unemployed Workers Movement
RILU: Red International of Labour Unions, Profintern
SDF: Social Democratic Federation
SL: Socialist League
SLP: Socialist Labour Party
SWSS: South Wales Socialist Society
TUC: Trades Union Congress
WSF: Workers' Socialist Federation

1.
Beginnings

The founding of a communist party in this country was an event of major importance in the history of the labour movement, and much has been written on its origin and subsequent development. To go over again the ground already covered in minute detail by such historians as Pelling, Macfarlane, and Klugmann[1] is not only superfluous but would be destructive of the purpose of this book, which is to present as clear as possible a picture of this party's political evolution over a period of time. What we are here concerned with is the party's political reaction to events and the extent to which this expressed or failed to express revolutionary socialist principles; that is, the broad course taken by the party 'line'.

The forces that made up the first contingents of the Communist Party of Great Britain (CPGB) naturally did not spring into existence overnight. Numerically the largest contingent of the new party was the British Socialist Party (BSP), which could trace its ancestry back to the Social Democratic Federation (originally, in 1881, the Democratic Federation) founded in 1883. The leading light of this organisation, H.M.Hyndman, had been a frequent visitor to Marx's household and in 1881 he published *England for All*, which, as Marx put it, 'pretends to be written as an *exposé* of the programme of the Democratic Federation, a recently formed association of different English and Scotch radical societies, half bourgeois, half proletaires . . . his little book, so far as it pilfers the *Capital*, makes good propaganda, although the man is a "weak vessel".'[2] In 1884 Engels wrote that the Social Democratic Federation (SDF) had succeeded 'in reducing the marxian theory of

A*

development to a rigid orthodoxy, which the workers are not to work their way up to by their own class feeling, but to swallow instantly without development, as an article of faith'.[3] This organisation did useful work but never quite broke out of its rigid orthodoxy while the Hyndman element dominated. When the Labour Representation Committee, forerunner of the Labour Party, was set up by a conference of trade unionists and socialist organisations in February 1900 in order to establish a 'distinct Labour group in parliament' the SDF was a part of it: but they did not appreciate what a great step forward this was for the workers' movement.[4] Unable to get acceptance by the new body of 'clear-cut scientific class-war socialism' (a worthy effort) the SDF decided to withdraw its delegates. The decision (Annual Conference, 1901) was taken by 54 votes to 14, showing some disagreement on the issue. Conditions were moving the organisation, albeit slowly, away from its dogmatism. The workers had awakened from their 'long winter sleep' during the period of colossal industrial growth between 1848 and 1880. The New Unionism at the end of the century had organised masses of hitherto neglected unskilled workers. In 1893 the Independent Labour Party (ILP) had been founded; it made rapid progress. The SDF was obliged to change its hitherto negative attitude towards trade unionism or be left stranded. At the 1897 Annual Conference an executive resolution was passed recommending all members to join unions and co-operative societies; in 1902 this attitude was re-affirmed, with greater precision.

In due course the organisation also recognised the need for a gathering together of all the socialist forces; and in 1911 it convened a Socialist Unity Conference, which was attended by delegates from ILP branches, Clarion groups,[5] and other socialist bodies, resulting in the formation of the British Socialist Party. Effectively, however, this was the old organisation under a new name, with some slight increase in membership. The outbreak of war in 1914 found the BSP divided on the issue of support or opposition; but the pro-war minority under Hyndman controlled the party organ, *Justice,* thus making it appear that the party as a whole was pro-war. The ensuing bitter internal battle culminated at the first wartime conference of 1916 in the secession of the Hyndman faction, leaving the international socialists in control, with their new paper *The Call*.

The British Socialist Party affiliated to the Labour Party in 1916 and its delegates were present at that party's annual conference in 1917. When the Bolsheviks took power in October 1917 the BSP gave the Russian workers' revolution unconditional support and expressed its firm belief in the inevitability of world revolution in the immediate future. After the founding of the Communist International (Comintern or CI) a party referendum decided by an overwhelming majority to seek affiliation.[6]

Second in numerical size, but no less important, were the recruits brought to the CPGB by the Socialist Labour Party, an organisation centred mainly in Scotland that had also evolved from the SDF, through a split in 1903. The SLP had adopted a version of syndicalism formulated by the American socialist Daniel De Leon, one of the founders of the Industrial Workers of the World (IWW), which was bitterly opposed to craft unionism and sought to organise all those employed in a particular industry into one union, eventually fusing all industrial unions into ' One Big Union ' which, by means of a general strike, would overthrow the existing order and conquer power. At its inception the IWW did not reject political action; but it did so in 1908, adopting tactics akin to anarcho-syndicalism, and De Leon broke with them.

The SLP published in pamphlet form a number of De Leon's writings and speeches. In *The Socialist Reconstruction of Society* (the title given by the SLP to a speech delivered in 1905)[7] De Leon expounds his view of the role of political action. 'It does not lie in a political organisation, that is, a party to "take and hold" the machinery of production.'[8] This could only be accomplished 'through an economic organisation of the working class, without affiliation to any political party'. The use of the ballot, electioneering ('the political movement bows to the method of civilised discussion: IT GIVES A CHANCE TO THE PEACEFUL

SOLUTION OF THE GREAT QUESTIONS AT ISSUE'[9]),
was a necessary tactic, but one wholly subordinate to industrial
unionism. In proclaiming the supremacy of the 'economic organisation' over the 'political organisation' the 'danger of rendering
. . . the labour movement illusory, and a roosting place for the
"intellectual" riff-raff of bourgeois society' was allegedly averted.
The political movement had a purely destructive aim, that of
'tearing down the political burg of capitalist tyranny'; it could
therefore 'not even remotely partake even of the appearance of
compromise'. On the other hand, the economic movement might
'take a little at a time' (i.e. presumably, seek to achieve 'transitional' reforms).

This teaching of De Leon had the merit of focusing the attention of the SLP on the work of agitation and organisation 'at the
point of production', although it had also the demerit of strengthening 'anti-parliamentarianism', a sectarian disregard of the actual
level of political consciousness achieved by the great majority of
the workers. Those attracted to the doctrine of industrial unionism
were, however, naturally those trade unionists with some degree
of political maturity, convinced socialists with a grounding in
marxism, who recognised the impossibility of getting 'a fair day's
pay for a fair day's work'. Their agitational and propagandist
activity would bear fruit during the war, when the industrial workers would turn to them for guidance, and make them leaders of the
shop stewards' movement.

The history of the shop stewards' movement has been dealt
with thoroughly by James Hinton in *The First Shop Stewards'
Movement*;[10] and an account of it as seen by one of the leaders,
J.T.Murphy, is given in *Preparing for Power*.[11] Wartime demands
on the productive process, giving a further powerful impetus to the
concentration of capital, and the rapid introduction of new tech-
niques rendering un-skilled and semi-skilled workers capable of
performing even more of the tasks hitherto the province of 'crafts-
men', confronted the workers with problems that demanded urgent
action, which the cumbersome, bureaucracy-ridden trade-union
machinery could not provide. Moreover, the top union officials'

major concern was co-operation with the government in its effort to maximise production. And rents and prices were rising as the patriotic landlords, employers and speculators did their best to maximise profits. In these circumstances only a rank-and-file organisation with a rank-and-file leadership could cope; and only the anti-war socialists could provide leaders bold and resolute enough to withstand the pressures of wartime 'public opinion' and governmental persecution. Many of the leaders in this wartime struggle were members of the Socialist Labour Party. With their experience of militant mass action in the industrial field, they were to be valuable recruits for the future communist party.

In addition to the BSP and the SLP two other organisations of lesser weight were involved in the founding of the CPGB – the Workers' Socialist Federation (WSF) and the South Wales Socialist Society (SWSS). The former was an offshoot of the women's suffrage movement so viciously persecuted by the Liberal government of the time. It was led by Sylvia Pankhurst, one of the band of dauntless warriors in what may be termed the 'direct action' wing of that movement – the Women's Social and Political Union. Appalled by the conditions of life and labour in the East End of London – 'that immense haunt of misery' (Engels) – which bore with particular severity upon the women-folk, Pankhurst turned towards socialism, and organised the Workers' Socialist Federation, with its organ, the *Women's Dreadnought*, later renamed *Workers' Dreadnought*. The WSF was anti-parliamentarian, did not correctly appraise the various levels of political consciousness among the workers and believed it possible to steer a straight, undeviating course to the revolutionary goal. On the other hand, it was internationalist in outlook, anti-war in a non-pacifist, international sense, and had considerable influence among the working women of the East End and the coal-miners of South Wales, whose strike struggles were given support and sympathetic encouragement by the *Workers' Dreadnought*.

The South Wales Socialist Society was a relatively small body, a flowering from the unremitting strife between coal-miners and coal-owners in that area, together with the marxist teachings of the Plebs League[12] and the propaganda of BSP and SLP members.

A variety of other socialist groups also responded to the call for revolutionary unity, all more or less oriented in the marxist direction. Among these were members of the Independent Labour Party, of the National Guild League[13] and the Herald League (formed to promote sales of and support for the *Daily Herald*[14]).

It is therefore clear that those who came together in 1920 and in 1921 to form the CPGB, were for the most part deep-rooted in the native soil of the labour movement; and also that they represented as a whole (regardless of individual idiosyncracies or shortcomings), in their general activity and thinking, the highest degree of political awareness then attained by any section of that movement.[15]

Throughout its existence the Communist Party has been bedevilled by the problem of a Labour Party enjoying the overwhelming support of the working people. What should be the attitude of revolutionaries to this party? It was this difficult and vitally important question that for some time held up the formation of the CPGB. William Gallacher, a member of the BSP in Glasgow, was one of those strongly opposed to any association with reformists. He wrote later about this:

> In 1920 I got appointed by the comrades in Glasgow associated with the Clyde Workers' Committee shop stewards' movement to attend the Second Congress of the Communist International. We were at the time 'left' sectarian and refused to participate in the discussions taking place between the BSP and the SLP on the question of the formation of a Communist Party in Great Britain.
>
> We had the project in view of starting a 'pure' Communist Party in Scotland, a party that would not in any circumstance touch either the Labour Party or parliamentary activity.[16]

The Glasgow group had refused to attend the first unity negotiations that, spurred on by the CI, took place between representatives of the BSP, the SLP, the WSF and the SWSS, as a result of which unification had been in principle agreed upon and a decision reached to prepare for a 'Unity' Convention. Before this took place, Pankhurst's WSF stole a march on the others and proclaimed itself the Communist Party, and the SLP split on the issue of affiliation to the Labour Party, those favouring this course establishing themselves as the Communist Unity Group. The Communist Unity Convention was finally held in London on 31 July and 1 August 1920.

The convention was attended by 152 delegates with 211 card votes. Pankhurst's organisation was not represented. Arthur MacManus[17], the chairman, referred in his opening remarks to the fact that the 'convention synchronised with the arrival of the Bolshevik commissars, who had now for the first time been openly invited by the British government'. Kamenev[18] and his comrades were expected that evening he said.[19]

The following letter from Lenin (dated 8 July) was read to the delegates :

Having received the letter of the Joint Provisional Committee of the Communist Party of Britain, dated June 20, I hasten to reply in accordance with their request that I am in complete sympathy with their plans for an immediate organisation of a Communist Party in England. I consider the policy of comrade Sylvia Pankhurst and of the Workers' Federation in refusing to collaborate in amalgamation of the British Socialist Party, Socialist Labour Party and others into one Communist Party to be wrong. I personally am in favour of participation in parliament and of adhesion to the Labour Party on condition of free and independent communist activity. This policy I am going to defend at the Second Congress of the Third International on July 15 at Moscow.

I consider it most desirable that a Communist Party be speedily organised on the basis of the decisions and principles of the Third International, and that that party be brought into close touch with the Industrial Workers of the World and the shop steward committees in order to bring about their complete union.

These two issues – the attitude to be adopted towards parliament and the Labour Party – evoked intense discussion at the convention. The resolution on parliamentary activity read :

The Communist Party repudiates the reformist view that a social revolution can be achieved by the ordinary methods of parliamentary democracy, but regards parliamentary and electoral action generally as providing a valuable means of propaganda and agitation towards the revolution. In all cases such representatives must be considered as holding a mandate from the party, and not from the particular constituency for which they happen to sit. [An amendment to add the word 'valuable' was agreed; and an addendum provided for the resignation of any elected candidate violating the party mandate.]

Moving this, Thomas Bell (SLP, Communist Unity Group) said that while they did not place any faith in the parliamentary institution itself, and did not believe that it was capable of fitting into the scheme of things that they as communists had in mind, nevertheless they thought it of considerable value as a means of liberating 'the minds of the masses from their superstitious faith in parliamentary democracy'.

A cruder approach was made by Robert Williams (BSP) who said that he had had the opportunity of discussing matters with Lenin and Chicherin (then Commissar for Foreign Affairs), and argued that 'it would be a considerable accession of strength if we had only one man in the House of Commons today who every time a cabinet minister got up to make a statement, would repeat: "You're a liar".' A remedy against the corrupting influence of parliament advanced by another BSP delegate was that every candidate should sign an application for the Chiltern Hundreds and hand this to the party executive, who would have only to fill in the date should an elected candidate prove unworthy. He supported parliamentary activity because, by obstructive tactics, parliament could be used to great effect. They did not want men who would go there to ameliorate the conditions of the workers, but men whose object was to smash the machine.

The resolution was passed by 4650 votes to 475 (186 cards against 19); those voting against being adherents of syndicalism proper, that is, totally rejecting parliamentary politics. Further discussion was then permitted on amendments. William Mellor[20] (Guild Communist Group) took exception to the proviso that the 'tactics to be employed . . . must be laid down by the party'. 'It seems to me,' he said, 'that the clause as drafted would lead to centralisation of the worst possible type, endangering local initiative and setting up a bureaucracy which future conferences would always be criticising.' Ellen Wilkinson[21] (a Guild and also an ILP member) retorted that 'if we are going in for a revolutionary party we must have a general staff and be willing to obey it'. After the revolution there could be local decentralisation, but in the meantime a revolution meant discipline and obedience. Another delegate put the point that, since under the Soviet system it was the people and not the party that had the right to recall an elected representative, it would be going too far in paternal government for the party to undertake to keep them in order. Many other speakers displayed strong antagonism to centralisation, which they equated with bureaucratic control.

Replying to these objections, Bell argued:

> Supposing, for instance, the Communist Party wants to cripple the constructive and administrative side of capital, and for that purpose decided that the elected members in parliament should immediately pursue a policy of destructive tactics there, and that those tactics should be supplemented by equally destructive tactics by members of local bodies, what the resolution provided for was that in those circumstances the executive should go to the members, state the policy of the party, and not only ask but expect them to endeavour to put it into operation.

By suggesting that 'centralisation' involved no more than insuring that elected representatives carried out party policy, the concern voiced about the danger of bureaucratic leadership was made to appear unwarranted. No one could deny that it was the duty of all members to carry out party policy. But Bell's argument really side-stepped the problem that lay behind this legitimate fear of bureaucratic control: how was this danger to be averted, how could centralised leadership with absolute authority be prevented from becoming authoritarian? Many if not most of those present thought more in terms of an administrative council rather than of an authoritative executive; although, as events would show, there was in general no very precise concept of the organisational structure required by a communist party. However, the party would before long have to deal with this matter and we shall see how it did so.

Sharper divisions were clearly revealed in the discussion on the second major issue before conference, affiliation to the Labour Party. The delegate moving the motion in favour of affiliation argued that the same arguments advanced in support of participation in electioneering applied equally to the affiliation issue. Inside the Labour Party 'we can use a lever by which we can ultimately destroy the influence of the treacherous trade union leaders on the political field'. Lenin, in his *Left-wing Communism: An Infantile Disorder*, had shed 'a flood of light on the whole question'. The Bolsheviks had shown the way to tackle these problems.

A week or two before the outbreak of the October revolution the Bolsheviks were getting ready their lists of candidates for the Duma [Constituent Assembly]. A fortnight, or it might be three weeks or a month after, they abolished the Duma. That is the way to be flexible. That is the way to adjust oneself to circumstances.[22]

Opposing the motion, William Paul (SLP) said that although he greatly admired Lenin, he did not consider him either a pope or a god : 'on international affairs we will take our principles from Moscow, where they can be verified internationally; but on local affairs, where we are on the spot, we are the people to decide.' Here it did not make any difference what Lenin said; those in favour of affiliation were required to prove their case by argument, not by appeal to authority. R.Page Arnot (National Guild League, Communist Unity Group) felt that the moment had not yet come when they could be perfectly sure that in splitting off from the Labour Party they could take a large body of the organised workers with them. Bell, on the other hand, thought that they would not necessarily be cutting themselves off from the workers if they refused to affiliate. In support of this view he pointed out that two of the delegates present had been elected to local councils 'on a strictly Bolshevik programme' without any help from the Labour Party.

The voting on this motion – 110 for affiliation, 85 against – showed the strength of the minority. Not even Lenin's very persuasive argument in *Left-wing Communism* had been able to wean them from their 'ultra-leftism'. True, he had admitted having 'too little information' on the issue of affiliation or non-affiliation – 'which is especially complicated on account of the quite unique composition of the British Labour Party, which is so unlike the composition of the usual political parties on the Continent' – but he went on to say that even so, his general argument applied here, too. Quoting the view put forward by Pankhurst in the *Workers' Dreadnought*, he had written that it would be a mistake to draw up the tactics of the revolutionary proletariat on the principle that 'the Communist Party must maintain its doctrine pure and its freedom from reformism inviolate; its slogan must be to go forward without stopping or turning aside, to follow the straight road to the communist revolution'.

Without doubt Lenin's role as persuader and teacher was considerable. The part played by others should also not be overlooked: Radek, Bukharin, Zinoviev and Trotsky were responsible for drafting important theses for the second Congress of the CI, with the purpose of educating the new parties (the role of the party in the proletarian revolution; the trade-union movement, factory councils and the CI; the communist parties and parliament). The extent to which the basic tenets set forth in these documents were absorbed is of course another matter; and in any event, those who did absorb them would in due course find – like all those who lived into the reign of Stalin – that the party had no room for them. All the parties, all the sections of the CI, from the mighty Russian to the tiny British, whatever their original composition, in whatever manner they had been formed, would in due course pursue policies and serve purposes very different from the ones for which they had been created. What follows will make clear how this process of transformation was effected and how it expressed itself in the politics of the Communist Party of Great Britain.

The new Communist Party quickly attracted other small groups that had not taken part in the Unity Convention. Carrying out a pledge made in Moscow, Jack Tanner and Dave Ramsay of the Shop Stewards' and Workers' Committee Movement, together with Gallacher and Murphy, used their influence to this effect at a conference in Leeds in January 1921. Shortly afterwards a number of ILP members joined, among them S. Saklatvala, a member of the wealthy Tata family of Bombay, and J.Walton Newbold (both were to become MPs, the former remaining a staunch but independent party member to his death, the latter becoming a MacDonald supporter). By the end of 1921 a broad-based communist party had finally been created.

2.
The Party of a New Type

Looking back on his first introduction to revolutionary politics, one of the early recruits wrote that 'when I first met the work of the CP, what an enormous difference there was between the old type of political party and the outlook, organisation and activity of this "party of the new type".'[1] In truth, however, the 'party of the new type' did not exist at that time, and the difference between the old and the new was not nearly so great as Dobb later imagined: for when he joined the CP in 1922 it was undergoing a thorough reorganisation, precisely in order to transform it into the new type. This reorganisation was being carried out on the insistence of the Comintern, in accordance with a resolution passed at the Third Congress in 1921.

Thomas Bell wrote of this resolution as follows: 'incidentally, while this resolution was modelled on thorough Bolshevik principles, as Lenin subsequently remarked at the Fourth Congress of the CI it followed too closely the Russian experience and methods.'[2] Lenin in fact went considerably further than Bell's comment indicates. His actual words were:

> At the third congress in 1921 we adopted a resolution on the structure of communist parties and the methods and content of their activities. It is an excellent resolution, but it is almost exclusively Russian, that is to say, everything in it is taken from Russian conditions. That is its good side, but it is also its bad side, bad because scarcely a single foreigner – I am convinced of this, and I have just re-read it – can read it. Firstly, it is too long, fifty paragraphs or more. Foreigners cannot usually read items of that length. Secondly, if they do read it, they cannot understand it, precisely because it is too Russian... it is permeated and imbued with a Russian spirit.

Thirdly, if there is by chance a foreigner who can understand it, he cannot apply it . . . My impression is that we committed a gross error in passing that resolution, blocking our own road to further progress. As I said, the resolution is excellent, and I subscribe to every one of the fifty paragraphs [in fact 59]. But I must say that we have not yet discovered the form in which to present our Russian experience to foreigners, and for that reason the resolution has remained a dead letter. If we do not discover it, we shall not go forward.[3]

In spite of Lenin's obvious dissatisfaction with the form of the resolution, since it had been passed there was nothing he could do about it. In any event, the content was sound. As he added, somewhat despairingly:

The foreign comrades must learn to understand what we have written about the organisational structure of the communist parties, which they have signed without reading and understanding. This must be their first task. That resolution must be carried out. It cannot be carried out overnight . . . The resolution is too Russian, it reflects Russian experience. That is why it is quite unintelligible to foreigners, and they cannot be content with hanging it in a corner like an ikon and praying to it . . . They must digest a good slice of Russian experience. How they will do this I do not know . . . We Russians must also find ways and means of explaining the principles of this resolution to the foreigners.[4]

One gathers that Lenin had no desire to impose this structure on the parties whether they understood it or not. Yet the resolution, which he characterised as 'excellent' and at the same time as 'a gross error' (or 'a great mistake'), must be carried out. It is difficult to reconcile the two views, unless one accepts that he thought it a great mistake for the parties to accept this excellent structure simply because it had behind it the authority and prestige of the Russians and not because they understood the spirit with which it must be imbued, and without which it would be worse than useless.

By 1922 the ebb of the revolutionary wave had left the British party in very low water indeed. The ebb, however, was not recognised as such by the Comintern. It was considered that the British party had been unable to take advantage of favourable objective conditions only because its organisation and activity was not appropriate to a revolutionary party.

The post-war boom, with its concomitant of wild speculation and inflation (the 1914 pound sterling's purchasing power had dropped by 1919 to 8s 8d, by July 1920 to 7s 9d) began to collapse in April 1920. By December the number of registered unemployed was 691,103; by March 1921 it was 1,355,206; by June 2,171,288 (17.8 per cent); by December 1,934,030 (16.2 per cent); and in December 1922 it was 1,431,929 (12.2 per cent). These figures minimise the actual unemployed, since they record only those covered by unemployment insurance. Many hundreds of thousands had to seek 'outdoor relief' from the Poor Law Guardians (the peak figure was 1,065,000 in June 1922), and some were refused. In September 1921 George Lansbury and 21 other Labour councillors in Poplar were all jailed for paying out too much. The Labour Party programme called for 'Work or Maintenance', but the right-wingers in that party (such as Clynes, Morrison) were of course outraged by this flagrant defiance of the law.[5]

Unemployment was particularly severe in shipbuilding, iron and steel, engineering and building: in December 1921, respectively, 36.1 per cent, 36.7 per cent, 27.2 per cent, and 20.5 per cent. It also hit some areas very much harder than others – Northern Ireland, Scotland, the Midlands and North East.[6]

In these circumstances, it was relatively easy for employers to comb out militants; but by the time the party had been formed the heart had gone out of the industrial rank-and-file movement and there was no prospect of an immediate revival of mass activity even where party activists had kept their jobs. For all effective purposes the shop stewards' movement had collapsed.

The party reaction to this situation was a shift of organised activity towards the unemployed and the established trade-union machinery. Reorganisation of the CPGB was, however, an effort inspired by the Comintern, whose *Theses on the Structure of Communist Parties and on the Methods and Content of their Work* applied to all parties. Following the Third Congress of the Comintern, and as a direct result of its deliberations on the British political situation, a party policy conference was called to discuss reorganisation. This conference took place in March 1922. It was then decided to set up a special commission to draw up a plan of reorganisation on the basis of the Third Congress resolution. This commission was composed of R.Palme Dutt, H.Inkpin (brother of the party secretary, Albert Inkpin), and Harry Pollitt, then London organiser of the newly formed British Bureau of the Red International of Labour Unions (the RILU) which subsequently developed into the Minority Movement, one of the many 'auxiliary' organisations run by the party. Pollitt, although hitherto not prominent in the party, was already well known in the Boilermakers' Society as an aggressively minded trade unionist. A former member of the BSP, he was strongly influenced by this party's tradition of working within the Labour Party. Hot-tempered, pugnacious, and at the same time not lacking in personal charm and homespun humour, Pollitt was also a very capable organiser and an impassioned agitational speaker. These qualities, plus a willingness to accept Comintern directives without reservations, were to assure his steady rise in the party. From 1922 onwards he battled for the top party post of general secretary, and in August 1929 he achieved his aim. Palme Dutt, son of Swedish and Indian parents, was a graduate of Balliol College, Oxford and worked in close harness with Pollitt, analysing the political situation and expounding the 'party line' as editor of *Workers' Weekly* and *Labour Monthly*. From 1927 on, both of them gave unqualified support to Stalin, whom they apparently regarded as a political genius second only to Lenin.

The report of the 1922 commission, drawn up by Dutt, was submitted to the Fifth Party Congress in October 1922. It was explained:

> A considerable portion of our first six weeks was taken up with working out detailed measures to meet the situation by cutting down headquarters expenses and so on. As a result of our recommendations the permanent staff at headquarters was reduced to one secretary, one organiser, and two clerical assistants.

Reference was also made to 'drastic measures in order to prevent a serious breakdown', and one of these measures was to reduce membership fees to a flat rate of one shilling per month per member. This particular change was effected on 1 July, and the reason for it was that a large part of the membership consisted of unemployed, who had previously been exempted from paying dues. Large-scale unemployment had seriously affected party members, particularly those prominent in the rank-and-file leadership of the engineering shop stewards. Many – foremost among them Wal Hannington and Harry McShane – turned to organising the unemployed, with great success.

The changes made prior to the congress were, said the report, 'temporary changes', made necessary by the urgency of the party crisis.

The party's inability to pay its own way would not have so much concerned the Comintern if better results had been shown for the money spent. As already noted, the Comintern did not accept that the circumstances of the time were unfavourable; they maintained that lack of progress was due to poor organisation and inadequate leadership. However, the effect of Comintern subsidies had itself made for a certain laxness in financial matters, which in turn contributed to a lack of drive in the general activity. Echoing Comintern criticism, the report stated that

> The Party has now been in existence for two years. They have been years of tremendous happenings, of great revolutionary significance, and of world-wide communist impetus. On every side the workers have been disgusted and disillusioned with the treachery of the old official leaders and have turned eagerly for new guidance. Yet in these two years, with all these opportunities, and with the tireless activity and energy of individual workers, the Party has made no real progress either numerically or in terms of influence.

It was argued that the main cause of the failure to make progress lay in the organisational structure of the party. A 'moderately active and efficient branch' of the party could be described as follows :

> The branch consists of about twenty members (this is the average for the country). Of these, half a dozen do the work and are probably accused by the remainder of being a 'clique'. Another half a dozen occasionally put in an appearance and lend a hand. The remaining eight are seldom seen; and of them the secretary is 'not

sure' whether they are still members, as he only has their names from the previous secretary's list ... The branch activity consists mainly of a weekly business meeting and a weekly Sunday morning propaganda open-air meeting.

This kind of unit would have to be abolished and replaced by a 'smaller unit of the actual working group, and the larger unit of the directing district centre'. The district centres and the national leadership would have in the future to closely direct all the activities of the members, each of whom would be allocated specific tasks and organised into a working group. Activity would need to be constantly tested by results; that is, by 'demonstrable increase of the party's influence', such as increased membership, circulation of literature, and the 'winning of sympathisers and contacts, or securing control of organisations'.

The executive committee would henceforth have to be in permanent session, 'instead of being scattered all over the whole country, and unable to meet except at long intervals'. Each member of the executive would direct and control a special department of activity, with the assistance of a Leading Committee. In this way, all work 'in trade unions, trades councils and local labour parties, in workshops, on local government bodies, and in general propaganda, etc.' would be co-ordinated, and the party converted into 'a single fighting force under a single leadership'. The report continued :

This is the vital secret of the Theses [the organisational theses of the Third Congress of the CI] that there is no rank and file in a communist party; every member has his specially allotted work and responsibility ... Every member has some special qualification which can be used in some sphere of the party's work. Each group by the nature of its work is gathering to itself new persons who are interested in its work. The group as rapidly as possible takes them in as candidates for the party; as soon as they become candidates they are allocated to special training groups to learn what the party stands for and so in course of time, with careful attention, they become full members of the party. In this way recruiting for the party is a constant accompaniment of all party work ... Our task is ... to create an efficient machine of the class struggle, capable of organising the entire working-class movement for the struggle, of confronting and battling with the complicated and centralised apparatus of the state, and eventually taking in hand the organisation of production itself. In all the smallness of our present conditions and difficulties we need never to let our thoughts fall below the magnitude of our tasks.

It is therefore not surprising to find the report saying:

> If an analogy were wanted to the position of the communist party centre, it would have to be found in the organisation which it is created to combat – the capitalist state. In the face of all the other dissimilarities there are the same basic principles of centralisation and specialisation – of many threads leading up to a departmentalised executive.

In order to effect the proposed change, the executive committee of the party would have to be chosen from the entire membership by the highest body, the congress, from nominations made at the congress.[7] Since the executive committee was to be in permanent session, its members would have to live near the party headquarters. The federal system of election, deriving from the manner in which the party had been formed from groups that had established themselves in different parts of the country, would have to be dropped. Henceforth the executive would be divided into two sections: the Organising Bureau and the Political Bureau (known in party jargon as respectively the Orgburo and the Politburo); the former handling technical matters, such as records, finance, allocation of members to specific tasks, communications, circulation of directives, etc. and the latter directing political activities: general meetings and campaigns, work in the trade unions and workshops, parliamentary and local government work, and so forth. These changes, it was said, would conform the party to the Russian model.

The method of party work in the industrial field was explained thus:

> The Factory Committee must not be confused with our own nucleus in the factory or workshop, or with any grouping of sympathisers around our nucleus which constitutes an advanced section in the workshop. The Factory Committee is a committee elected by all the workers in a given enterprise, without distinction of union, craft organisation, or other special condition. The Factory Committees are the mass organisations of the workers, that unite all the workers,

irrespective of political opinions, for the common struggle, developing into the conscious struggle of the working class for power. In the majority of cases a Factory Committee will only be thrown up in some actual crisis, and we must be ready to seize the opportunity when it comes: but our agitation for the formation of a Factory Committee goes on all the time, and makes use of all occurrences and grievances that may arise to point in this direction.

It is here envisaged that Factory Committees will normally only be thrown up spontaneously as a result of some particular 'crisis'. (Later, however, in particular when an open, all-out effort was being made after 1929 to establish the party as an immediate alternative to the Labour Party, the creation of such committees became the party's constant concern. Early endeavours to 'build the party on a factory basis' had resulted in the publication of a number of factory sheets. These, although not ostensibly issued by the party, publicised the party's agitational 'line'. Experience showed, however, that such sheets offered too narrow a basis, and they also exposed those publishing and circulating them in a given enterprise to reprisals on the part of the employers. They were therefore abandoned in favour of industrial news sheets, i.e. papers aiming at arousing support for demands of a 'transitional' character for particular industries, thus making it possible to co-ordinate action on a national scale. Examples of such papers were: *The Platform*, for bus workers; *Power*, for engineers in power stations; and *The New Builders' Leader*.)

The need to base the party on the factories is referred to in party literature with ever-increasing frequency from 1922 on. *The Report of the Seventh Congress* (1925) contains the following statement on this subject:

> *Organisation on the basis of factory groups is the characteristic and specific form of Bolshevik organisation, in distinction from the organisation of the reformist parties.* [emphasis in original]. Their territorial organisation is adapted to the needs of the parliamentary struggle, i.e. of 'normal' peaceful times. The factory organisation is adapted to the needs of a Bolshevik party, working in the 'abnormal' times of the breakdown of imperialism, the use of White Terror, etc. Territorial organisation (whether working directly or through trade union branches) gives access only to the small active minority

of the working class (and then only the *organised* section of the working class), whereas the factory organisation connects the party directly and permanently with the *mass* of the workers, organised and un-organised. The territorial organisation tends to divorce the party members, still more the party officers, from the mass of the workers; factory organisation brings them into and makes them part and parcel of the life of the workers. Territorial organisation concentrates the attention of the party upon the workers as scattered individuals or residents, and tends to blur the distinction between them and the petty bourgeoisie. Factory organisation, on the other hand, not only turns the main party attention upon the workers, but also focuses it upon their most class-conscious and decisive section grouped in the largest factories and workshops. 'The large factories contain the predominant section of the whole working class, not only in numbers, but still more in influence, development, capacity for struggle' (Lenin in 1902).

An essential aim laid down in the 1922 report on re-organisation was the establishment in every workshop of a hard core of party members, referred to as a 'nucleus' (later the word 'cell' was more generally used), which would seek to win the leadership of broadly based committees to direct the struggle against the management.

An observation in the report on the question of workers' control deserves notice. This reads: 'It should of course be remembered that workers' control and similar formulae, etc. are not objectives in the struggle preceding the revolution but are only slogans or demands to develop the struggle, and so carry forward our propaganda.' Here the influence of the Russian experience is very evident: for the slogan of workers' control, expressing the revolutionary urge of the workers to shake off the employers' yoke in the period between the February and the October revolutions, was accepted by the Bolsheviks and used by them as a slogan to develop the struggle but not as a specific aim, and was quickly abandoned in favour of 'personal management of industry'. The report appears to assume that what applied to Russian conditions must necessarily also apply to Britain; however, in a highly developed capitalism workers' control must surely be seen as an essential objective of the revolutionary movement – the form of control necessary for the reconstruction of society.[8]

The activities of party members in trade unions, factories and other workplaces, were to be directed and supervised by an Industrial Department at headquarters, either directly, or through the medium of District Industrial Committees.

Operations in the industrial workplaces were to be supplemented by 'infiltration' of trade union branches. Work in both areas would appear to be complementary, but the report makes it clear where the main work had to be directed:

> The factory or workshop . . . is the real unit of the working class, and should be the main field of our activity . . . The trade unions only bring us into contact with a portion of the workers. The workshop brings us into contact with the whole working class. The trade unions only bring us into contact with the artificial groupings of the workers, and only the minority which turns up at branch meetings, etc.

From the standpoint of revolutionary socialist politics the correctness of this view cannot be questioned. Yet at the same time the report goes on to say that: 'The purpose of the party's work in the trade unions is to transform them into mass organisations of revolutionary class struggle under the leadership of the party.' It could of course be argued that the two approaches were complementary, but a fair portion of the party membership did not accept that a revolutionary transformation of the trade unions was possible. However, the Comintern had already set up the Red International of Labour Unions[9] and a British Bureau of this organisation had been established in 1921, with precisely this ostensible aim.

The 1922 report on reorganisation enjoined the Central Industrial Department to establish Advisory Committees for each of the principle unions or groups of unions. These would consist of the best members in the union concerned, who would meet and deliberate at party headquarters, or the headquarters of the union itself, should this already be under party control.

> Nuclei [i.e. party cells] need to be organised in any trade union branch where we have one or two members. A trade union nucleus is a party organisation working in any trade union branch . . . A nucleus only exists when it has been organised by or reported itself to its Leading Committee, and is meeting, working, and reporting

regularly. The nucleus will receive full instructions as to its work at the time when it is formed by the representatives of the Leading Committee accredited for this purpose, and thereafter will receive particular instructions over any issue or campaign as occasion arises.

This ensures tight control by the leadership over rank-and-file activity together with maximum effectiveness. Since party members in a given trade union branch are pursuing a line of action planned in detail beforehand, and all other members in other branches are doing the same, this gives them an obvious advantage over opponents whose activities are not so co-ordinated. The fact that all party members can be swung into action simultaneously on any given issue makes for the most effective use of the forces available. The method has not, for reasons that this study will make clear, served to extend revolutionary consciousness among the workers, but it has proved its technical effectiveness in promoting party members to leading positions in some unions.

The report details the work of the party cell in a trade union as follows:

In addition to the special issues and campaigns that may arise in their union, they will have regular day-to-day work to do which is common to all nuclei in trade union branches. The nuclei will endeavour to increase attendance at its branch and develop interest in union affairs; it will organise left-wing opposition in its branch around all current questions, or seek to gain control of it where one already exists; it will be prepared for each branch meeting with resolutions, movers of resolutions, discussion, and so on; its members will take cases of victimisation, compensation, and other local grievances, and so win confidence by active personal assistance; it will endeavour to weaken the position of reactionary officials and leaders by pressing issues which force them to take up an unpopular stand; it will aim at pushing the rules to their limit, and so expose their unwieldy character, and work for their alteration; it will work for the election of accredited communist candidates as officials and delegates to conferences, and so on; during strikes its members will be active in the forefront and pressing for the extension of the dispute and greater solidarity, and it will be watchful to keep the Leading Committee informed of all developments and to follow carefully the lead given in order to achieve uniformity in the party's action.

At higher levels – district committees or executive committees of unions – party members will equally be organised into cells, which will meet and report regularly, and receive their instructions from the Leading Committee. 'Officials in a union will be separately organised for party purposes, and will have to furnish their own reports regularly on their work, together with any information obtained, and will receive their instructions.'

It should be noted that members of the Central Industrial Committee – i.e. the directing body for party industrial and trade-union activities – are not chosen because they represent any particular industry or union, but because of their 'communist understanding of the work as a whole'. This is because all such activity is theoretically wholly subordinate to, and conceived of as a contribution to, the political objectives of the party. However, difficulties have inevitably been encountered in the application of this principle. Party members elected to official positions in trade unions are not elected because they are communists, but because of their aggressive, 'militant' championship of the workers' economic demands. One has only to note that those very same trade unionists who vote for party members as officials vote for the Labour Party when it is a matter of 'politics' – with rare exceptions in the past, which only went to prove the rule. Moreover, union officials – even those professing to be communists – tend by virtue of their status as officials to take the view that it would be pleasanter to stay in office than go back down the pit or whatever. And to do so, they have to take account of the militant workers who elected them. Thus a conflict of interest may arise and a communist official may refuse to toe the party line if he feels that this will prejudice his standing with the workers. A particular instance of this will be seen in the party's conflict with Arthur Horner, considered later. The likelihood of such conflict receded, however, as the party settled down to a policy of 'left' reformism.

In this 1922 report the trades councils were regarded as being somewhat in the nature of potential soviets. Formed originally as local strike committees, they had since been 'increasingly relegated to the background in the labour movement'. They could, it was argued, become 'invaluable means of party propaganda, providing opportunities for bringing under our influence the local organisations and securing control of the direction of the local movement'. In order to achieve this it was necessary here, too, to establish 'fractions' which would 'meet separately before the trades council meeting to go through the agenda, propose resolutions, arrange movers and seconders, etc.' Reports of members' activities on the trades councils would be given either to the District Industrial Committee or in default of such, to the centre, from where the Central Industrial Committee would direct the work as a whole.

> The fraction on the trades council will in the first place use all the opportunities provided by the trades council for furthering and extending the scope of the party's propaganda. This applies particularly to the opportunity for propaganda among the affiliated bodies.

Control of a trades council would make it possible to send party speakers and lecturers to affiliated bodies.

The question of the party's attitude towards local government bodies is disposed of in the report in the following forthright manner:

> The Communist Party does not enter on local government bodies to help in their work but to expose and destroy them as part of the bourgeois machinery of administration. For this purpose the work on them must always be subordinate to the objects and tactics of the mass struggle outside.

The broad objective here is to 'expose the class character of local government and lead to open conflict with the central authority'. The existing situation, said the report, where party members elected to these bodies were acting purely as individuals, required immediate attention.

Only tentative reference was made to the question of work in the Labour Party, since this matter was not within the province of the party commission on reorganisation. However, it was stated that should the party decide to continue to work in the local Labour Party organisations, such work would have to be conducted by the same 'fraction method' as used in the trades councils. In the event, the party did decide to continue to 'work in the local Labour Parties'.

The Annual Conference in October 1922 endorsed the report on reorganisation and the party now stood equipped with the technique considered essential to its transformation into 'the party of a new type'. A great deal of thought had gone into the production of this model organisation and it is incorrect to assert that the Comintern's intention was to transform the parties into 'bureaucratic instruments of revolution'.[10] A paragraph in the Comintern resolution on organisational structure points out that

> There can be no one absolutely correct and unalterable form of organisation for the communist parties. The conditions of the proletarian class struggle are subject to change in an unceasing process of transformation and the organisation of the proletarian vanguard must always seek the appropriate forms which correspond to these changes. Similarly, the parties in the different countries must be adapted to the historically determined peculiarities of the country concerned.[11]

However, this is somewhat qualified by the following paragraph, which speaks of 'definite limits' to this differentiation, similarity of the conditions of the class struggle creating a common basis for organisation. In the event, the 'common basis' dominated, to the exclusion of the 'peculiarities', but the bureaucratic degeneration of the parties, including the British, was not caused by the organisational structure itself, although this was used to facilitate the process; used, in the event, in the very spirit against which the Comintern resolution had warned in the following passage :

> Centralism in the communist party organisation is not formal and mechanical but the centralisation of communist activity, that is, the formation of a strong, militant, and at the same time flexible leadership.
>
> Formal or mechanical centralisation would be the centralisation in the hands of a party bureaucracy of 'power' to dominate the other members or the masses of the revolutionary proletariat outside the party. But only enemies of communism maintain that the party wants to dominate the revolutionary proletariat by its leadership of the proletarian class struggle and by the centralisation of this communist leadership. That is a lie. Equally incompatible with the principles of democratic centralism as adopted by the Communist International is a conflict of power or a struggle for domination within the party.

> The organisation of the old non-revolutionary labour movement developed an all-pervading dualism . . . the dualism between bureaucracy and 'people'. Under the ossifying influence of the bourgeois environment their officials became estranged and a living labour community replaced by a purely formal democracy and the splitting of the organisation into active functionaries and passive masses. To a certain extent, the revolutionary workers' movement has unavoidably inherited this tendency to formalism and dualism from the bourgeois environment.[12]

The problem is, how to ensure that this dualism does not come about? How does one realise Lenin's injunction that 'the revolutionary "staff" must be genuinely supported by the honest and conscious will of the army, which follows its staff, but at the same time *directs* its staff?'[13]

It is clear that everything depends on the spirit and calibre of the 'army', which in turn depends on or can be affected by environmental pressures. And the CPGB was subject not only to the pressure of its native bourgeois environment, but also to the pressures from the Russian environment.

The CPGB at its inception had more than enough of the spirit capable of resisting bureaucratisation. Its founding brought together those most conscious of the gulf between democracy of the letter, formal democracy, and democracy of the spirit and the deed; those most uncompromising in their opposition to arbitrary authority, to careerism and all self-seeking. The party was almost exclusively proletarian in character (too much so, in fact; with the added disadvantage of 'anti-intellectualism'); its members had reached their appreciation of the social order more through their experience of working-class life and labour, than from theory. This was their strength, but also their weakness. Constant preoccupation with agitational activity on a hundred and one issues left little time for study and discussion of political issues that were being fought out in Russia, even if the inclination for this had existed and even if the documents, the necessary information, had been made available, which they were not. However, the need for such information and discussion was recognised by only a handful; for the rest, with their markedly anti-intellectual bias, theoretical discussion tended to be regarded as time-wasting, holding up the action. There were, of course, good grounds for regarding intellectuals with suspicion; their record in the parliamentary labour movement offered damning evidence of opportunism and careerism.[14] But wariness is one thing, almost total rejection quite another, making it all too easy for the professional functionaries to stifle awkward discussion of policy. This anti-intellectualism in the CPGB, translating itself into impatience with critical discussion, was probably the main reason why opposition to bureaucratisation found so little response among the rank and file.

Left to sort out its own problems – not without guidance and advice from the Comintern; not without studying, and learning from, the experience of other parties; but without the obligation to follow undeviatingly the line laid down from above – the CPGB might well have developed towards a party commensurate with the economic and social conditions of the times. But paragraph 46 of the Comintern resolution on party structure contained a sentence that obliged the CPGB, willy-nilly, to carry out any policy decided upon by the Comintern. This sentence ran: 'Directives and decisions of the International are binding on the party and of course on every individual member'. There was nothing inherently bad about this proviso – *given that there actually existed a revolutionary world party, genuinely democratic, with 'staff' and 'troops' an integral whole, in which a struggle for power was unthinkable, domination by any one section impossible.* This remained no more than an intention, although there is ample evidence in the proceedings of the first congresses that every effort was made to realise the aspiration. The forces of counter-revolution were too powerful; the revolutionary internationalists were defeated; nationalism took over. And, in the words of a founder member of the French CP, Charles Rappoport, 'Nationalism is a religion, the most tenacious and the most dangerous of all. No other religion has cost humanity so much blood and tears; so much cruelty and misery.'[15]

3.
A Rope for the Labour Party

Having accepted Lenin's advice on the immediate tactical course to be pursued vis-à-vis the Labour Party, the provisional executive elected at the 1920 Unity Convention applied for affiliation in a letter dated 10 August. The letter stressed the principled differences between the two parties, pointing out that communists rejected parliament as an instrument for achieving socialism and championed the soviet system and the dictatorship of the proletariat as the only possible road to this objective. In his history of the party, Bell wrote that 'some of the comrades were inclined to think that the letter was too sharp and rather calculated to invite rejection by the Labour Party'.[1] Allen Hutt, an acid critic of Bell's book, admits that 'sectarianism marked the party's first approach to the Labour Party', but maintained that the case presented was nonetheless sound.[2]

Replying to the application, the Labour Party argued that 'the basis of affiliation to the Labour Party is the acceptance of its constitution, principles and programme, with which the objects of the Communist Party do not appear to be in accord'.

It is possible, even probable, that the crude manner of the party's first approach to the Labour Party was due not so much to a lack of finesse as to the still strong feeling against having anything at all to do with the reformists. Even for those wholly convinced of the correctness of the affiliation tactic it was certainly not thought of as a long-term matter. The revolution was in the offing; there was a vision of a brave new world before the eyes of these angry, hopeful young people; soon, very soon, the hucksters of the political market-place would be chucked into the dustbin of history.

The Labour Party Conference held 27-30 June 1922 at Edinburgh, rejected the CP's application for affiliation by 3,086,000 votes to 261,000. It heralded the process of expelling communists from the Labour Party, and the unions. It looked as if the affiliation issue was dead. Arguing on these lines at the Fourth Congress of the CI Murphy proposed that the attack upon the reformist fortress must therefore be carried out by means of the 'open' infiltration tactic, which was already, he claimed, showing excellent results. In Glasgow, Sheffield, Manchester and Birmingham their influence was so strong that the Labour leaders had been unable to make their resolutions effective. 'Furthermore, in other places, Barrow, Battersea, and other local Labour Parties the communists have practically got control of the Labour Party organisations.' A telegram received at the congress, and read out by Zinoviev, announced the election of J.Walton Newbold to parliament for the Motherwell constituency; he had stood as an avowed communist.[3] This gave support to Murphy's view that affiliation now no longer mattered. A direct effort must be made to win over the Labour Party rank and file to communism.[4]

A number of factors made possible the successes of this 'open' penetration, but possibly the most important was the sentiment widespread in the labour movement that communists 'belonged' to the movement – they were fellow fighters in a common battle. True, the Edinburgh conference had accepted a constitutional change making communists ineligible as delegates; but the very nature of the Labour Party structure, making for a high degree of local autonomy, made this decision largely inoperable in default of strong measures from above. So it was that at the next Annual Conference there were 38 communist delegates, as against only 7 the previous year. However, the vote in favour of communist affiliation (in spite of Murphy's contention that the issue was dead, it continued to be pressed) rose by only a small amount, to 366,000. The Edinburgh decision making communists ineligible as delegates was withdrawn. This expressed trade-union reluctance to impose a political qualification upon members and also reflected a growing left-wing mood in that quarter, arising from the general trade depression.

Once more the capitalist social order was manifesting its inability to control the productive forces it had itself developed.

The 1924 Annual Conference of the Labour Party, meeting in a pre-election atmosphere, upheld the decision of the previous year regarding the eligibility of communist delegates. But on many questions of the relationship of communists with the Labour Party there was an evident confusion of thought, as the following voting shows:

1. That the application of the Communist Party for affiliation be refused: carried by 3,185,000 to 193,000.

2. That no member of the Communist Party be eligible for endorsement as a Labour candidate for parliament or any local authority: carried by 2,456,000 to 654,000.

3. That no member of the Communist Party be eligible for membership of the Labour Party: carried by 1,804,000 to 1,540,000.

Thus, although affiliation was rejected even more decisively than in 1922 – marking a set-back on the 1923 vote – the vote supporting communists as Labour candidates was up by more than 300,000 on the 1923 affiliation vote. Even stranger than this was the extremely narrow margin by which communists were excluded from membership of the Labour Party. Perhaps the most convincing explanation for this apparent confusion is that the trade-union left-wingers made a distinction between communists as individuals and the CP itself. The CP was the avowed enemy of the Labour Party – the two sets of principles and programmes diametrically opposed – but communists as individuals were, after all, stout fighters in the trade-union struggle. Quite a number of them had long and proud records in that struggle and all were active in the recruitment of members to the unions. The right-wing could quote telling passages from CP and Comintern pronouncements, couched in terms calculated to offend more than to persuade and demonstrating beyond doubt the hostility of the CP to the Labour Party; but that was politics and not to be taken all that seriously.

What mattered was the trade-union struggle. Then again, the communists were in favour of a Labour government; they would urge the voters to vote Labour.

Another consideration that no doubt weighed with some trade-union leaders, and affected their attitude towards the communists, was the question of trade with the Soviet Union, which would alleviate the effects of the depression on their members. This may well have induced some to adopt a tolerant attitude towards those who were, so to speak, the 'accredited representatives' in Britain of the Russian revolution. Moreover, the communists were a small and ineffectual band whose diatribes against the Labour leaders should not be taken too seriously.

But there was more than tolerance of this kind, there was in the broad labour movement still a feeling of fellowship towards communists. George Lansbury expressed it when he wrote:

> The *Daily Herald* up to 1922 . . . supported the claim of the communists to be allowed to affiliate with the National Labour Party. We never disguised the fact that the communist methods were not ours, but we looked on them, few or many, as part of the workers' movement, and as such entitled to affiliation.[5]

The Communist Party's persistent attacks on the Labour leaders, their 'boring from within' via the Minority Movement[6] in the trade unions (which was, of course, denounced by the reformists as 'disruptive'), and the effect on the electoral prospects of the Labour Party of the so-called Zinoviev Letter (see below), led to a hardening of the opposition to them at the 1925 Annual Conference of the Labour Party. An executive recommendation that no member of the party should be eligible for membership was this time carried by 2,870,000 to 321,000 votes; and an appeal to trade unions not to elect communists as delegates to Annual Conference was accepted by 2,692,000 to 480,000. This led the CP to organise its members and sympathisers inside the Labour Party into a National Left-wing Movement. At the inaugural conference of this body it was reported that '65 groups had been established; 24 in London, 6 in Wales, 5 in Lancashire, 9 in Yorkshire, 11 in Scotland, 4 in the Midlands, 3 in naval ports, and the remainder in other parts of the country'.[7] As a result of the activities of this body, 60 of its members were present at the 1926 Annual Conference of the Labour Party at Margate. After the General Strike the CP claimed that it had (in November 1926)

> something like 150 groups and fractions all operating within the Labour Party, and this is by no means the complete total. In London alone, we have 87 fractions as compared with 30 a year ago. Sixty-five of these operate and report regularly as compared with twelve a month ago. Forty-eight Labour parties have endorsed the Left-wing programme.[8]

At the second conference of the National Left-wing Movement in 1927, and again in the following year, it was claimed that 1,455 members of the CP itself were 'active' in local Labour parties, and that 252 communists had been elected by trade union branches as delegates to local Labour party management committees. Thus, in spite of some counter-measures (13 local Labour parties were in 1926 disaffiliated for refusing to expel communists), the 'open' penetration tactic could claim successes. However, all this was geared to agitation for a 'fighting' Labour government, which could only serve to sustain the very illusions the CP was trying to destroy.

It must be constantly borne in mind that the CPGB was not, even at this stage, entirely free to make its own mistakes. Any consideration of communist politics must be not only incomplete but also meaningless if it leaves out of account the decisive influence exerted by the Russian leaders, by Russian politics. The rein may have at first not been tight, not even felt by the membership, but it was nonetheless there.

When Zinoviev, at the Fourth Congress of the CI (1922), said that more attention should be paid in future to the CPGB, the word attention meant more than the dictionary definition of 'concentration of the mind upon an object'. At this congress a 'resolution on the reorganisation of the CI towards an International Communist Party' was passed (later published as a pamphlet by the CPGB). One clause of the resolution read:

In special cases the Executive shall send a delegate to the individual countries, who shall be drawn from the most highly qualified comrades of the sections. These representatives shall be endowed by the Executive with the most comprehensive powers. In special cases the functions of these envoys, their rights and duties, and their relation to the party in question, shall be precisely set down in writing.

The Executive is empowered to supervise with special emphasis the effective application of the 21 conditions and the execution of decisions of the world congress. The envoys are to be explicitly entrusted with this supervision. The envoys must report on the results of their work at least once a month.[9]

The policy to be followed by each section of the Comintern was decided at the world congresses, decisions being based on the findings of 'commissions' composed of representatives of various national sections: a British commission would be made up of representatives of the British, German, French, Italian and Russian parties. In theory such decisions were based on an objective analysis of the situation in the country in question and on exhaustive discussion of the commission's findings. In the early years such discussion was in fact normal. National peculiarities were recognised and tactical flexibility accepted within the framework of the strategic 'general line'. Even so, the dominance of the Russian party was apparent at an early stage. A further provision of the above-quoted Fourth Congress resolution was that 'No less than 15 members of the Executive must be permanently domiciled in Moscow' (out of a total of 24, plus the president). The German party delegate and member of the Executive, Eberlein, refuted 'enemy' charges of Russian control and argued that

the Russian comrades on the presidium and the ECCI must be accorded the greatest weight, for they have the greatest experience in the field of international class struggle; they are the only ones who have really carried out a revolution and they are therefore far superior in experience to all delegates from other sections . . . But it is essential for the other parties to collaborate more and more in running the CI, and to send their most able representatives.[10]

The prestige of the Russian leaders did not in those days stifle criticism but it gave their views a weight hard to resist. In addition, there was the almost insuperable difficulty of holding international congresses without the material assistance the Russians could offer, and the direct financial dependence of many parties.[11]

As a section of this world party, the CPGB was obliged to publish and circulate statements of the ECCI, even though they might prove more embarrassing than helpful. A resolution of 6 February 1924, expounding the Comintern's attitude towards the Labour government ran, in part:

> If (we do not expect it) it should become possible to drive the Labour government by proletarian class movements into a fight with capitalism, the internal crisis in England would thereby be rendered extremely acute. But if, as is to be expected, the Labour government betrays the interests of the proletariat, it will thus offer the best possible object lesson to the proletariat, enabling it to free itself from the illusions of capitalist democracy, and will thereby accelerate the revolutionising of the working class.

The resolution went on to urge the communists in Britain to 'assist' the workers to convince themselves of the 'utter worthlessness of the Labour leaders, of their petty-bourgeois and treacherous nature, and of the inevitability of their bankruptcy'. The way to do this was by 'supporting the Labour government's programme', but at the same time pressing forward 'other immediate slogans calculated to mobilise the class-conscious sections of the working class for common action'. For its work to be effective, the CPGB must 'maintain its ideological, tactical, and organisational independence', while trying to 'come to agreements for such and such common action with "left" political organisations, as well as with local organisations of the Labour Party'.

This ECCI resolution was in the nature of a corrective to the CPGB's first flush of enthusiasm at the result of the general election of 1923 – an enthusiasm shared also by the Moscow press, not to speak of the entire British labour movement. In the December 1923 general election Labour won 191 seats (against 158 Liberals and 258 Tories). In January 1924 a minority Labour government was formed under Ramsay MacDonald. It lasted till the general election of October 1924 when the Tories returned to power.

At the top level of the labour movement there were three views as to what should be done with Labour's electoral 'victory': one, that of MacDonald and company, who wanted to take office at all costs and show how well they could govern; the second, advanced by Lansbury,[12] Kirkwood,[13] Smillie[14] and others, of absolute opposition to a minority government dependent on Liberal support; the third, expressed by Maxton,[15] Thomas Johnston (editor of the Scottish *Forward*) and others, of supporting only a Labour government that would at once put forward proposals so uncompromisingly socialist as to lead to immediate defeat and a fresh appeal to the electorate. The CPGB wavered between the first and third views, writing to the Labour Party to express satisfaction at the electoral success and declaring its readiness to assist the Labour Party to the utmost of its ability. 'Our guiding principle must always be *the workers against the capitalists*. On that principle we are with the Labour Party in taking office', declared the *Communist Review* in February 1924. And Dutt had written in the *Labour Monthly* of January that a minority government could not be expected to show immediate results but that the workers would understand. So long as the Labour government stood clearly for the workers against the capitalists it was a duty to support it 'no matter whether they agree with its programme or not'.

It was of course very difficult for the communists themselves not to be infected with the jubilation and elation that then filled the hearts of every class-conscious working man and woman; but the CPGB's response brought them perilously close to socialism on the parliamentary never-never system. The Russians' own initial enthusiasm waned rapidly and, as noted above, the ECCI resolution brought the CPGB back to earth.

The Labour government was given no time to demonstrate conclusively its impotence to solve the capitalist crisis: its life was cut short by the Campbell affair. This arose from an effort of the CPGB to give effect to the fourth of the *Twenty-one Conditions* of admission to the CI, which began: 'The obligation to spread communist ideas includes the special obligation to carry on systematic and energetic propaganda in the army'.

On 25 July 1924, the *Workers' Weekly*[16] published an open letter addressed to the armed forces, calling upon the 'workers in uniform' to 'organise passive resistance when war is declared, or when an individual dispute involves you'; to 'form committees in every barracks, aerodrome or ship'; and concluding with the summons to 'Turn your weapons on your oppressors!'. Taking into consideration that the British armed forces were composed of professionals and not conscripts and the relatively insignificant forces at the party's disposal it is not surprising that the communists had not been able to do any propaganda worthy of the name in this field. This appeal, as it were out of the blue, had therefore no more serious meaning than as an item for the CPGB's Comintern record. That it may also have been calculated to challenge prosecution by the Labour government is suggested by the fact that the editor of *Workers' Weekly*, Dutt, was absent at the time, and that the acting editor was J.R.Campbell, a war veteran who had been severely wounded and decorated for gallantry. In any event, the exercise can hardly be considered a serious attempt to educate the workers in the armed forces.

As a result of this article the premises of *Workers' Weekly* were raided by the police and Campbell was arrested and charged with an offence under the Incitement to Mutiny Act of 1795. Maxton raised the matter in the House of Commons, but the Speaker ruled it *sub judice* and therefore not open to discussion. There was immediate uproar from the Labour back-benchers, incensed at this attack on free speech and the freedom of the press. Some threatened that they too would go to their constituencies and publicly express the same view as those contained in the *Workers' Weekly*. If all those ready to do this were arrested, charged and found guilty, said one of them, the Labour Party would lose half its MPs.

The CPGB threatened that if the case was pressed they would put MacDonald in the witness box. Among other matters on which the Prime Minister would be questioned was his House of Commons speech on 4 June 1912 in which he had eloquently defended Tom Mann, then accused of advising soldiers not to shoot strikers.

The prosecution was dropped. The Opposition thereupon charged that the Labour government had yielded to pressure from the extremists in its ranks, quoting the communists' claim that a revolutionary victory had been won. The Tories and the Liberals combined to bring down the government.

In the general election that followed, the CPGB maintained its policy of supporting the Labour Party. The main issue was the Russian treaty and a loan to Russia, to which the Conservatives and many Liberals were violently opposed. Everything possible was done to depict the Labour Party as 'Bolshevik', strange as this may seem today. In Churchill's phrase, which put the Tory campaign in a nutshell, Labour, allied with the communists, was ready to 'shake hands with murder'. It appeared that Ramsay MacDonald was a revolutionary on a par with those monsters of iniquity Lenin and Trotsky. Perhaps a more telling illustration of the atmosphere of those years was the charge made against John Wheatley of the ILP in the House of Commons that he was making propaganda 'for those who preach the class war', when all that he had done was to describe life in the Glasgow slums and propose reforms. There could be no doubt that the ruling class sensed in the rise of the Labour Party a grave threat to its power; rightly so, for behind the Labour Party was a politically aroused mass, the overwhelming majority of the workers. The Bolshevik seizure of power in Russia was for the ruling class another dread omen. There was no knowing what might happen at home too, if the workers were not put firmly in their place.

This election campaign in an atmosphere charged with fear and hate on the one side, hope and elation on the other (throughout the land huge audiences responded with rapturous enthusiasm to MacDonald's oratory), brought an eve-of-the-poll shock. This was the discovery of a letter, apparently a directive from the Comintern, signed by Zinoviev and the British communist member of the ECCI, calling upon the CPGB to prepare for insurrection and civil war. It was a patent forgery, clearly designed to round off the anti-Labour campaign, summed up in the slogan 'A vote for Labour is a vote for Bolshevism'. The Labour vote not only stood firm, it even rose, but hordes of dare-devil voters who had previously plumped for the Liberals scurried back to the Tory fold.

The communist policy of 'supporting' the Labour Party was in all the circumstances essentially sound, but the tactic of 'penetrating' diverted activity from the party as such to the auxiliary 'Left wing' inside the Labour Party. What was the perspective of such activity? In 1924 Zinoviev was asserting that the British workers were rapidly becoming 'revolutionised' and predicting that 'the disintegration of the Labour Party is now inevitable'.[17] 'The next important task of the Comintern', he concluded, 'is to create a mass Communist Party in Britain.' Echoing this view, Dutt wrote that 'The revolutionising of the Labour Party means its disappearance, or even . . . its "liquidation".'[18] Communist policy had therefore to be based, not on the perspective of strengthening the Labour Party, 'but on building up the revolutionary mass movement within the Labour Party, which mass movement must develop the mass Communist Party'. From this it would appear that the main activity of the party had to be directed to the Labour Party, which would disintegrate' or 'disappear' or be 'liquidated' and give place to a mass CPGB. The grounds that Dutt gave for this optimism were: the growth of the influence of the Minority Movement in the trade unions; the Anglo-Russian trade-union rapprochement (of which the TUC delegation to Moscow was a symptom); the great increase in the circulation of the left-wing press (the *Sunday Worker* and Lansbury's *Labour Weekly* had, Dutt said, a joint circulation of 150,000 to 250,000); and the Labour Party executive's retreat on the question of the eligibility of communists as delegates to Annual Conference.

However, there were some British communists who disagreed with this highly optimistic view of the approaching demise of the Labour Party. The chief dissenter, J.T.Murphy, argued that, so far from 'decomposing', it was 'increasing in strength as the workers became more class conscious'. Consequently the task of the CPGB was to 'help the working class organisation . . . to shake themselves free of the control of bourgeois politicians'. Dutt charged Murphy with advocating the subordination of the Communist Party to the Labour Party, and there was no doubt some truth in this. The very existence of the CP imposed a handicap on the 'left wing' in the Labour Party. The tactic of infiltration and 'capture' would have a much better chance of success if operated by a left-wing body unhampered by the open existence of a British section of an international party that made no bones of its bitter hostility to the Labour Party. However strenuously this left-wing organisation denied control by the party, no one was deceived, since every success of this organisation had to be hailed by the party as a victory for itself. There was bound to be a certain amount of friction over how much attention should be given to one or the other field of work. It goes without saying that no one even dreamed that the CPGB should fold up, but if it was true that the Labour Party still had a long lease of increasingly vigorous life and that therefore work inside that party should be the communists' main concern, then the role of the CPGB would be diminished; there would indeed be the danger of its subordination to the Labour Party, of which Dutt warned.

The 1924 defeat of the Labour government naturally shifted the emphasis of working-class struggle to the industrial field. Here the party made some progress. In 1922 the book membership figures were 5,116, but of these only 2,300 regularly paid dues. The subsequent shake-up and reorganisation in that and the following year cut out the dead wood and prepared the way for growth. By 1924 a solid membership of 3,800 could be claimed. By 1925 this had risen to 5,000; by April 1926 to 6,000. As a direct result of the General Strike (see chapter 4) the membership jumped to 10,800; but a considerable proportion of this figure failed to be consolidated, so that by September 1927 membership had fallen to 7,377. These are official party figures and therefore not necessarily reliable, but they illustrate the general trend over these years, making clear the party's inability (frequently lamented by the leadership) to translate industrial influence, quite considerable before, during and after the General Strike, into political conviction. Still, by 1927 the party was firmly based and might look forward to steady progress.

Time showed that Zinoviev's forecast of the imminent 'disintegration' of the Labour Party and Dutt's forecast of its 'liquidation' were way off beam. The great majority of the workers continued to regard that party as their party. Moreover, since their severe defeats in the industrial field they had turned once again to parliament, to the prospect of electing a Labour government as a solution of their problems. The report of the Eighth Congress of the CPGB in October 1926, stated that

> the reformist leaders have advanced a step towards their aim of preventing the evolution of the Labour Party into a class organisation, and of transforming it into a definite Liberal Party, the 'third party of the capitalist class'. The decline of capitalism in Britain must ultimately defeat this policy, *so long as the Labour Party remains based on the trade unions*; but the control of the Labour Party machine by the reformists, through the present leadership of the trade unions and through the ILP is a powerful means of delaying the evolution of the Labour Party into a definite class organisation, and, therefore, of sabotaging the successful struggle of the working class.[19]

The only thing clear from this statement is that the reformist leadership had emerged from the General Strike strengthened, not weakened, and that their hold on the Labour Party machine must be broken. Apart from this, all is confusion. For a party to *remain* based on the trade unions, it must already be so based and must therefore be a basically class organisation; yet it is argued that it is only 'evolving' into a class organisation and that the aim of the reformists is to prevent this : at that time the Labour Party was somewhere in the no man's land between a class party and 'a definite Liberal Party' (but that too is a class party, representing the aspirations of capitalists and the middle class).

The true situation was that the Labour Party had been established to represent the interests of the workers organised in trade unions, interests that the Liberals, hitherto trusted by the workers, had demonstrably betrayed. With the growth of the Labour Party it had become infiltrated by all kinds of careerists, its original basic working-class character diluted but by no means destroyed. It became precisely the aim of the reformist bureaucracy to destroy this working-class character, to create the image of a party representing the 'nation'; that is, to reconcile the irreconcilable, to satisfy all interests in the interest of its own political advancement. But however much the Labour reformists would like to be shot of the unions, they knew it could not be done, for without them there would be no Labour Party. So they constantly hoped and prayed that the trade-union bureaucracy would be able to keep their membership on a tight rein. The key to the problem of how to shake the workers' faith in reformism thus lay primarily in the industrial struggle, among the rank-and-file trade unionists.

After the Margate conference of the Labour Party, Pollitt crowed that the executive could not 'disqualify a trade unionist, who is a member of the Communist Party, and elected by his trade union as a delegate to a Labour Party conference'.[20] The CPGB was spending a great deal of time and energy on this kind of victory. The small ground gained – if it could be viewed as such – was soon lost. The Labour Party executive began to take vigorous expulsion measures, evoking the protest from J.R.Campbell that 'this policy . . . has disgusted and driven out of the Labour Party hundreds of good workers who were not communists, but who were not prepared to take part in the cowardly, capitalist-inspired heresy hunt'.[21] One would need to be pretty innocent to be deceived by this disingenuous concern at the loss to the Labour Party of 'hundreds of workers'. But again there is confusion. The implication is 'Look what your leaders are doing! They are weakening the Labour Party by their witch-hunt against us communists, which causes hundreds of non-communists to resign their membership.' Where, then, did the CP stand? Did it or did it not consider the Labour Party an obstacle in its path? What were those 'good' workers good for? Had the CP not been trying to bring those good workers to communism, or had they been trying, and failed?

It was not entirely the fault of the CPGB that it could not

make up its mind where it stood in relation to the Labour Party. Its mind was being made up for it by the Comintern, and the Comintern was undergoing a process of change that would finally wipe out the last vestige of its original revolutionary intent. This process took place over a relatively short period and was an integral part of the triumph of the counter-revolution in Russia. One aspect of it was the attempt by the Russian leaders to affect a rapprochement with the British trade unions, through the so-called Anglo-Russian Committee, which we shall now consider.

4.
'All Power to the General Council'

The Red International of Labour Unions had been set up and the British Bureau established in 1921 in order to attempt to transform the trade unions into revolutionary organisations. But the British Bureau in due course displayed a tendency to 'duplicate what was . . . the function of the Communist Party',[1] – in other words to evade party control and become in some degree a rival body.[2]

This situation, together with the failure of the British Bureau to make any headway with the direct campaigning for union affiliation to the RILU, and the general lack of progress by the party in circumstances regarded by the Comintern Executive (ECCI) as relatively promising, led to a special commission on the CPGB, in Moscow, in June 1923, on the occasion of the Third (enlarged) Plenum of the ECCI. Ten extra delegates from the party's top leadership were invited to this special commission, or conference. As a result of the discussions held, the British Bureau was phased out in favour of an effort to bring together existing rank-and-file groupings on the industrial field, and to set up new ones wherever possible.

Out of this there eventually came the National Minority Movement (NMM), which held its formation conference in August 1924. Basing itself on the appeal of limited economic ('transitional') demands, the NMM rallied a very considerable body of support. According to the Fifth Comintern Congress resolution on the British Labour government, the task of the British party in relation to the NMM was to:

a. support the left in all their actions against the trade union bureaucracy, in strikes and in propaganda ...

b. reinforce the solidarity of the Minority Movement and mobilise it on a national scale around a programme based on the platform of the RILU;

c. strengthen the Minority Movement by the struggle for the creation of factory cells and so lay the foundations for industrial unions with the factory cells as the basic union organisation.[3]

However, in 1924 the Russian party also introduced into the British trade-union scene the tactic of the united front 'from above'; a tactic that eventually brought the communists into a 'fraternal alliance' with the top trade-union leaders, many of whom were puffed up by the party as potential recruits to the revolutionary cause. Hence the party slogan of 'All Power to the General Council' that expressed communist policy during a most crucial period of working-class struggle in this country.

Whatever the original intention may have been in the consciousness of the communists, this alliance became an attempt to find a short cut to the masses by winning over their leaders, thus skipping the spade-work of winning over the rank and file to the revolutionary cause.

The Labour government of 1924 took office pledged to establish diplomatic relations with the Soviet government and open up trade negotiations. In spite of the very evident timidity of Ramsay MacDonald, arrangements were made for an Anglo-Soviet Conference to consider questions outstanding between the two countries, and in due course a Soviet delegation arrived in England. On 14 March the TUC, which saw trade with Russia as a means of easing the economic depression and fervently desired the success of these negotiations, invited the trade-union members of the Soviet delegation to a dinner. After A.A.Purcell, president of the TUC, had delivered a speech of welcome, M.I.Tomsky,[4] chairman of the All-Union Central Council of Trade Unions (AUCCTU), set forth the Soviet attitude on the question of the tsarist debts, trade and other matters. In the course of his speech, he made flattering reference to the Soviet Union's indebtedness to the precedents established by the western unions, especially the

British. He asserted that any differences between the two movements were superficial, a view from which no one present dissented. Ben Tillett expressed the sentiments not only of the TUC but of the entire labour movement when he said, 'There is not any one of us here whose sympathies have not gone out to Soviet Russia'. Fred Bramley, winding up for the TUC, said that full normal relations between the two countries must be achieved; economic progress in Russia would favour the same in this country and they all knew that if the conference failed the consequences for British labour would be very serious indeed.

This marked the beginning by the Russians of a tactic that was highly ambiguous, combining what appeared to be a genuine desire at reconciliation with the reformist unions with statements indicating the precise opposite. Hindsight makes it possible to see that this ambiguity was the expression of the struggle in Russia between the revolutionary internationalists and the counter-revolutionary exponents of 'socialism in one country'.

The Hull Trades Union Congress of September 1924 invited Tomsky to address it as a fraternal delegate. In the course of his address Tomsky said that if the Russian workers had been able to hold on to power, it was 'before all, thanks to the French and British workers, who had the manhood to say to all the world: "Hands off Soviet Russia".' He gave especial thanks to comrade Purcell, who had been the chairman of the Hands Off Russia Committee. To Cramp, of the NUR, who had expressed mild doubts about the Russians' motives, he gave a soft answer. The Profintern (i.e. the RILU) might be a good thing or it might be a bad thing, he said: 'a great many people do not like it; but the essential point is that it exists'. He knew that many of the British comrades thought that the Russians and the Profintern had been too severe in their censures on the leaders of the western European trade-union movement. Perhaps they had. But the way to put an end to these disputes was simply to make one international of the two. 'Simply bear in mind that there are more than seven million organised workers in the Moscow International.'

He insisted that the Russian unions had tried again and

again for unity. 'You have an outstanding position: you may almost be regarded as the rulers of the trade-union world; you are not merely super-Amsterdam, for you take command of the whole international trade-union movement.' It was enough for the British workers to say, 'Let there be unity', and there would be unity. This was greatly to exaggerate the influence of the British unions on the International Federation of Trade Unions (IFTU), which in the event would never go farther than a readiness to accept the affiliation of the Russian unions, which in effect meant closing down the Profintern. (According to Trotsky such affiliation was in fact conditionally advocated by Tomsky, and 'unconditionally and categorically by Kaganovich' in 1925. Trotsky also stated that in 1926, 23 Russian unions had 'changed their statutes in the sense of omitting the reference to their membership of the Profintern and substituting a reference to membership of an International Federation of Trade Unions'.)[5] The exaggeration was no doubt intentional flattery, but behind this was also a genuine respect for the organisational strength of the British unions.

Following this cordial exchange of compliments, the General Council sent a delegation to the Sixth Soviet Trade Union Congress in November – December, consisting of A.A.Purcell, Fred Bramley, Herbert Smith, Ben Tillett, John Turner, John Bromley, and A.H.Findley.

In a speech at a reception in honour of the visitors, Tomsky reiterated his argument that the Russian break with the western trade unions had been forced upon them against their wishes. 'January 1918, the first Trade Union Congress decided that the Central Council of Russian trade unions must establish connections with the trade unions of the west', but the blockade had prevented this. Moreover, at the Berne congress of trade unions in February 1919 (given as 1918 in the text), no desire to discuss with the Russian unions was expressed. 'That situation forced the Russian trade unions in 1921 to set about the formation of a new Trade Union International of our own'.[6]

This explanation of the formation of the RILU is not consistent with the facts. Right from the start the Bolsheviks had made no principled distinction between the political and the trade-union wings of the reformist organisations. The attitude taken up by the Second International on the outbreak of war in 1914 had been a gross betrayal of socialist internationalism. Henceforth the true international socialists could have no truck with such an International, but must seek to found their own. The need for an International of revolutionary trade unions appears as a logical consequence of the founding of the Communist International in March 1919.

Why then did Tomsky say that the split had been forced on the Russians against their wishes? Why did he forget that point 10 of the *Twenty-one Conditions* made implacable hostility to Amsterdam a matter of principle? Such a transformation was possible only because the revolutionary tide in Europe had ebbed, as a consequence of which the predominating view in the Russian party was that no immediate help could be expected from that quarter, and that Russia would therefore, for an indefinite period, be thrown back on her own resources. This correct view of the situation dictated a fresh tactical approach internationally. But another and quite different conclusion drawn from it was expressed in Stalin's theory of 'socialism in one country', proclaimed in the autumn of 1924. In Tomsky's case, ultra-pessimism about the revolutionary potential of the European proletariat expressed itself in an excessively conciliatory attitude towards the TUC leaders.

The Sixth Congress of the Russian unions passed a resolution stressing the need for international trade-union unity, which among other things stated:

> In this regard the Sixth Trade Union Congress considers that its duty is to identify itself with the intentions voiced at the Hull congress of the British trade unions, and notes with satisfaction that ... by the decision it has adopted it is meeting the wishes of the overwhelming majority of the British workers.
>
> With a view to co-ordinating the work of the British and Russian trade union movements in promoting unity, the Sixth Trade Union Congress hereby furnishes the Central Council of Russian Trade Unions with full powers, after the necessary negotiations with the

> General Council of the British Trades Union Congress, jointly to
> form an Anglo-Russian Committee whose task it shall be to co-
> ordinate the activities of the trade-union movements of both coun-
> tries in their struggle for international trade-union unity.[7]

In his pamphlet, Lozovsky writes that the British delegation
was hesitant to express agreement with this general principle, but
that the insistence of Bramley – 'a man of very moderate outlook
but with a clear head and a firm will' – won the others over. However this may have been, the official report issued by the British
delegation on its return showed few traces of criticism. The report
was the joint effort of the delegation's three advisory delegates,
H.G.Grenfell and A.R.McDonell (both former Foreign Office
officials), and G.Young (a member of the diplomatic service in
Russia from 1896 to 1915). It ran to 275 pages, with 19 full-page
photographs, maps and graphs. Its general tenor was not dis-
tinguishable from that of official Soviet propaganda. Petrovsky
(otherwise Bennett), the Comintern representative then attached
to the British party, wrote in appreciation of this report that it

> has played a powerful role in so far as it has strengthened among
> the British working class the position of the friends of the Soviet
> Union against the reformists of the Second and Amsterdam Inter-
> nationals. We should like to add that this report has made a power-
> ful impression even outside Great Britain.[8]

This report was therefore widely used for 'friends of the
Soviet Union' type of propaganda, and also as evidence of the
value of this kind of get-together at top level. Communist party
propaganda along these lines naturally also served the reformists
well, enhancing their 'left' image.

After some fruitless attempts to enlist the co-operation of
the continental leaders of the IFTU (Amsterdam), the General
Council convened a Russo-British conference to discuss further
ways and means of achieving international unity. This conference
took place in London (6-8 April 1925). Tomsky now asked if they
could not put on one side for a moment the things that divided
them, and try to find out the things on which they could find
common ground and on which they could unite. The IFTU

demanded that the Russians accept its constitution and rules; but that would mean that they must declare before the whole world that they broke with the RILU, and that they no longer had any concern for what happened to their friends, such as the left trade unions in France and other countries. That they could not do. All kinds of wild and foolish stories were being put about, to the effect that the Russian unions were out to disintegrate and corrupt the IFTU, to corrupt the labour movement of the west. That was all nonsense. They simply wanted to meet the leaders of the Amsterdam International; they were ready to be influenced by them – if that was possible. What was there to be frightened of in a mutual exchange of experiences? Tomsky went on to assure his listeners that the stage of abusing Amsterdam was over. Now the Russian and the British trade unions would together fight successfully for international trade-union unity.

All this had an appealing ring. Moreover the political and economic situation in Britain – the fall of the Labour government, the establishment propaganda equating the Labour Party with Bolshevism, the Zinoviev letter fraud, the persistent pressure for wage reductions, the plight of the unemployed – all contributed to a sharpening of class antagonism, and strengthened the argument for 'unity against the common enemy'. Among the workers the spirit of rebellion quickened; there was a sense of great battles impending.

At the Labour Party Conference of 1924 affiliation of the CPGB and endorsement of communists as Labour Party parliamentary candidates were both turned down by overwhelming majorities. But the resolution refusing individual communists membership of the Labour Party was passed by a mere 264,000 votes; indicating the strength of the feeling of fellowship with communists.

The CPGB and the Minority Movement were conducting a vigorous campaign for international trade-union unity, and were supported in this by such ostensibly left allies as Purcell, Cook and Hicks. From the standpoint of the rights, association with the Russian unions would invest them with a certain aura of leftism –

a useful counter to this pressure. So agreement was finally reached on the establishment of an Anglo-Russian Committee (ARC) for the sufficiently vague purpose of achieving 'international unity of the workers of all countries' as 'an impregnable force against capitalist oppression' and 'an unbreakable pledge of peace and economic security'.[9]

It can be recognised that this gave the General Council a means of warding off attacks from the left; but what precisely did the Russians hope to gain from it? From the Russian party discussions on the question of the ARC, the only thing that emerges clearly is that this 'getting together' was regarded as marking a breakthrough for Russia out of the isolation in which it had been placed by the 'stabilisation' of world capitalism; the first step on the road to a united front with the European working class; in Zinoviev's view, 'the greatest hope of the international proletariat'. But the degree of enthusiasm for this 'breakthrough' varied considerably, from the excessive optimism of Zinoviev to strictly qualified acceptance by Trotsky. There was no disagreement as to the legitimacy of making such an approach to the reformist leaders. In the course of events disagreement of a secondary nature arose between Lozovsky (representing the Profintern) and Tomsky (for the Russian unions), but the fundamental clash was between the Stalinist conception of this 'united front' and that of the Opposition, led by Trotsky. When it became clear that the bloc with the General Council was regarded, not as a temporary agreement designed to put the reformists to the test, but as an enduring partnership for the 'unity' of oil and water – then the Opposition called for the immediate breakup of the ARC. To maintain this bloc after the General Council had betrayed the General Strike was to collaborate in deception of the working class.

Already before the General Strike, Trotsky had made his position clear in *Where Is Britain Going?* This book, first published by the CPGB in February 1926, was issued in a revised edition in October, with a preface written on 6 May, six days before the General Strike was called off. The following extract from this preface illustrates the author's standpoint:

The general strike is one of the most acute forms of class war. It is one step from the general strike to armed insurrection. That is why the general strike more than any other form of class war, demands a clear, resolute, firm (i.e. a revolutionary) leadership. In the general strike the British proletariat shows no trace of a leadership of this kind, and it cannot be expected that it will appear all at once in a perfected form as if conjured out of the ground.

... the general strike ... if carried through to the end, brings the revolutionary class up against the task of organising a new state power. Nevertheless, those who by the course of events have been placed 'at the head' of the general strike are fighting against this with all their strength ...

We must look the facts straight in the face; the chief efforts of the official leaders of the Labour Party and of a considerable number of official trade-union leaders will not be directed towards paralysing the state by means of the strike but towards paralysing the strike by means of the bourgeois state ...

The strike itself cannot alter the position of British capitalism ... This requires the reorganisation of the whole of British industry. The strike is only an emphatic expression of this necessity ... A real victory for the general strike can only be found in the conquest of power by the proletariat ...

The key question in this strike, which Trotsky characterised as 'the greatest revolutionary movement of the British workers since Chartism', was obviously the question of leadership.

During the General Strike some of the communist leaders were still in prison. They had been arrested in October 1925 on a charge of seditious libel and incitement to mutiny, and sentenced to varying terms of imprisonment, under the Incitement to Mutiny Act of 1797: Pollitt, Gallacher, Hannington, Rust and A.Inkpin to 12 months; Campbell, Murphy and five others to 6 months. The political report of the central committee to the Eighth Congress of the party (16-17 October 1926) carried the comment that the prosecutions had 'acquainted thousands of workers with the principles of our party', and greatly assisted its recruitment campaign. (However, the Sixth Plenum of the ECCI in March 1926, while referring to the 'success of the CPGB in extending its influence and in capturing the leadership of the working masses', also noted its failure to translate influence into new membership.[10]) Government persecution undoubtedly gave a fillip to the party's morale and aroused widespread sympathy and support, obliging the TUC and the national executive of the Labour Party to pass a joint resolution condemning the government's action. The depth of feeling aroused can be gauged by the fact that even MacDonald moved a resolution in the House of Commons condemning the prosecutions.

If courage, self-sacrificing devotion and tireless energy were all that a revolutionary party requires, the influence and standing of the CPGB would have been enormously enhanced by the strike. But they are not enough. Unfortunately, the party did not adapt itself to the situation politically, but clung to the policy arrived at long before the strike – incorrect then, even more so when battle had been joined. This policy was the one supremely important factor deciding the effectiveness of party activity, regardless of its organisational weakness.

The way the CPGB looked at the situation is exemplified in J.T.Murphy's article in the *Workers' Weekly* of 30 April, where he wrote that

> Our party does not hold the leading positions in the trade unions. It can only advise and place its press and its forces at the service of the workers – led by others. And let it be remembered that those who are leading have no revolutionary perspective before them. Any revolutionary perspective they may perceive will send the majority of them hot on the track of a retreat. Those who do not look for a path along which to retreat are good trade-union leaders, who have sufficient character to stand firm on the demands of the miners, but they are totally incapable of moving forward to face all the implications of a united working-class challenge to the state. To entertain any exaggerated views as to the revolutionary possibilities of this crisis and visions of new leadership 'arising spontaneously in the struggle', etc. is fantastic.

To be noted here is Murphy's preoccupations with 'leading positions', the separation of the trade-union leaders into the good ones and the bad ones: the latter would scuttle off at the first sight of a revolutionary perspective but the former would 'stand firm' for the miners. This is all of a piece with the Anglo-Russian Committee line of thinking and the 'All Power to the General Council' slogan. These leaders, good and bad alike, are not, and never will be revolutionaries, so there must be no 'exaggerated views of the revolutionary possibilities of this crisis.'

Now, if by *'exaggerated* views' one intends to convey that a revolutionary overthrow of the existing order is out of the question, this can be freely granted. But in the passage quoted everything is made to hang on the non-revolutionary character of the trade-union leadership. They cannot be won over; so the crisis offers no possibility of a new leadership arising; so all that the party can do is to 'advise'. This is exactly what the party did.

That the workers were 'led by others' was precisely the reason why the party existed. This indisputable fact was interpreted as meaning that the workers were so hopelessly reformist that the crisis – and what a crisis! – would in no way shake them out of their accustomed way of thinking, that to propagate the revolutionary message would only alienate them from the communists (thus ignoring the fact that in February 1917 the Russian workers, too, had been under the spell of reformist illusions). As a consequence of this failure to recognise the revolutionary potential of the workers in a crisis situation, the party persisted in its compromise with reformism, advising the striking workers to trust the General Council, and further fostering reformist illusions by calling for 'formation of a Labour government'.

Of course there were others in the CPGB who differed with Murphy's analysis. Early in 1925 Dutt had urged criticism of left-wing leaders such as Hicks, Purcell, Cook and Maxton. After Red Friday (31 July 1925), when the miners' strike threat, backed up by the General Council's order for an embargo on the movement of coal, had apparently brought the workers victory over the government and the employers, Dutt wrote that

> the left trade-union leaders occupy at present the position, not only of the leaders of the workers in the immediate crisis, but also of the spokesmen of the working-class elements in the Labour Party – it might almost be said, an alternative leadership – in the present stage the language of the left trade-union leaders is the closest indication of the advance of the British working class to revolution.[11]

Dutt's estimate of the workers' mood was sound – as was

shown by their response to the strike call – but the conclusion he drew was not: he did not recognise that the left leaders were not leading but merely responding to the left mood of the workers; they did not and could not represent an alternative leadership. Murphy's underestimation of the workers' potential and Dutt's overestimation of the left leaders were two sides of the same coin and led to the same result: 'All Power to the General Council and the Formation of a Labour Government'.

The trade-union leaders had drifted into a situation that scared them out of their wits. Believing that Red Friday would be repeated, that the government would yield in face of the threat of concerted trade-union action, they had felt safe enough even to toy with revolutionary phrases, aware of the weakness of the communists. They had reckoned neither with the inflexibility of the government and their determination for a showdown, nor with the revolutionary spirit of the masses. Eventually the TUC General Council blundered their way into calling the General Strike at the urging of the miners, threatened by wage cuts. It was to last from 4 May to 12 May. When the two armies confronted each other, when the skirmishing threatened to develop into full-scale warfare, their bluster deserted them, their hearts turned to water. Rumours were circulating: they would all be arrested, trade-union funds would be impounded . . . Trilbies in hand, they went to No.10 and abjectly surrendered.[12]

The strike was absolutely solid, strengthening daily. All over the country the workers had demonstrated their ability to throw up fresh leadership locally, to invest with new, revolutionary content their old, long-established trades councils. The daily monotonous routine of workaday life was gone. Exhilarated by danger, by a sense of power, the dream of a brave new world now at last surely becoming real – they were now suddenly dealt this brutal blow by their own leaders!

They were totally unprepared. It was impossible, unbelievable, a government lie . . . When the truth of the desertion by their leaders sank in, there was great anger. Only this and the fighting spirit of the workers prevented the defeat from degenerating into a rout. The communists did what they could do to stiffen morale and for this deserve all praise. Not to be left out of account, however, is the large number of socialists – of the ILP, of the Labour Party, of those not attached to any party – who everywhere had risen to the occasion during the strike and now did everything possible to aid an orderly retreat. The employers were exultant, eager to take advantage of the situation and humiliate the workers, but the temper of the workers restrained them. Even so, victimisation was quite widespread.

It was a foregone conclusion that the General Council would betray. The CPGB warned of this – as a *possibility*, not as the certainty that it really was. They warned, half-heartedly, and then wiped out the warning by calling for 'All Power to the General Council'.[13]

After the strike Dutt wrote that 'the General Council representatives had already deserted the miners before the General Strike began', and that the trade-union leaders had 'entered the struggle with the one thought to find by one way or another the most rapid way out to call it off'.[14] Yet in this same pamphlet he continued to appeal on behalf of the party for the 'concentration of power in the hands of the General Council'.[15]

How can one account for this strange ambivalence? Before, during and after the General Strike the policy of the CPGB was vitiated by the need to support the ARC tactic. The task of the party was, in Stalin's words, 'to push forward and carry to the end the struggle for the unity of the trade-union movement, bearing in mind that this is the surest means of capturing the millions of the working-class masses'.[16] The ARC was regarded as a major step forward on the road to unity.

But, whatever the immediate purpose of a united front might be, the revolutionary party cannot separate this purpose from the ultimate objective of working-class power. Such a united front cannot be forged around an abstraction: 'unity' in general. It must have a specific, concrete objective, which may be to defend ground already won or to press forward to gain new ground. But the essential matter is that it puts the reformists to the test: are they or are they not prepared to fight for this objective? The ARC with its nebulous concept of 'unity' could not do this, it could only foster illusions. All that the British workers saw was that their leaders were in fraternal unity with the Russians, whose revolutionary prestige they did not question.

In 1925 the CPGB had a little over 5,000 members. Its influence was however considerably higher than this figure indicates, but it was an influence based on the appeal to trade-union militancy, that is, on the aggressive spirit it displayed in championing immediate economic demands; and on its organisational efforts among the unemployed. The very fact that the membership of the party had remained static during the five years of ever-mounting social unrest preceding the strike, showed that the party had not succeeded in putting across its message. Many hundreds of thousands looked to it for support in the struggle for immediate demands, but few joined the party; they did not look to it for *political* leadership. And, as the workers sensed, the General Strike was above all political in content. Even if one assumes that the period before the strike in no way favoured political progress by the party, that it would have failed to make such progress whatever its policy and tactics, it cannot be said that the General Strike situation itself did not offer an unprecedentedly great opportunity for the party to strengthen itself permanently and solidly.

The party emerged from the strike with its membership slightly more than doubled. The overwhelming majority of the new recruits came from the minefields, a tribute to the party's unceasing, determined and well-organised campaign in support of the miners' courageous struggle against the coal barons.

The CPGB had published Trotsky's book, *Where Is Britain Going?* in February 1926 and reprinted it in October, but had not understood it. The book had been

> aimed essentially at the official conception of the Politbureau, with its hope of an evolution to the left by the British General Council, and of a gradual and painless penetration of communism into the ranks of the British Labour Party and trade unions.[17]

The CPGB had not got the message. On the contrary, it had agreed offhand with the Stalinist proposition that opposition to the policy content (essentially reformist) of the ARC was 'defeatist'. It had shared the Russian Politburo's opportunist illusions (expressed also in China through the alliance with Chiang Kai-shek, the butcher of the Chinese communists[18]), and had consequently failed to impart revolutionary education to the workers. As a result even those meagre gains the party made from 'the greatest revolutionary movement of the British workers since Chartism' were insecure. This was already demonstrated in April 1927 in the diminished support of the conferences organised by the Minority Movement (in furtherance of the party's totally unrealistic campaign for a renewed General Strike against the government's anti-trade union Bill)[19] and in the drastic drop in representation at the Minority Movement's national conference that year (from the previous year's 950,000-odd to 300,000). By the end of 1927, 30 per cent of the CPGB's membership gains had already been lost.

5.
Stalinisation of the CPGB

The Ninth Congress of the CPGB took place in October 1927. No radical change of policy was then effected. On the contrary, support for a Labour government was re-affirmed, together with the tactic of applying for affiliation to the Labour Party. In February 1928 the central committee published a thesis on this long-established policy, in order to 'afford scope for a frank and full discussion throughout the party'. In this thesis it was stated that

> Our present attitude towards the Labour Party is fundamentally determined by the fact that the British Labour Party, in spite of its social-democratic programme, its 'completely putrefied leadership' (Bukharin's speech at the Fifteenth Congress of the CPSU) and the attempts of its leaders to impose social-democratic discipline, is not yet a social-democratic *party* in the accepted meaning of the term . . . owing to its trade-union basis, the communists can still enter the Labour Party 1) as trade union delegates to the committees and conferences (for selecting parliamentary candidates) of local labour parties; 2) as trade-union delegates to the Labour Party Conference; 3) where communist influence is strong, as parliamentary candidates of the trade unions (the Lanarkshire Miners' Union and comrade W.Allan).

It was further argued that the 'present policy of the party was based to a considerable extent on the advice given to the party in 1920', and that it was 'a mistake to argue that Lenin's advice is obsolete on the ground that he gave it in a different situation from that existing today', because the 'tempo of revolution is not even as high today as he described it in June 1920'. By working within the Labour Party and exploiting all the opportunities it gave for propagating communist views, the CPGB had, it was claimed, 'extended its influence at a time when an isolationist policy would have killed it'. Further,

> the adoption of a policy within the Labour Party which alienates mass support from our Party would also alienate support from us in the trade unions, the majority of the members of which still look to a Henderson-Cook government.

To oppose candidates that had the backing of the local labour movement would only serve to raise a barrier between the communists and the mass of the workers supporting the Labour Party, whom it was their duty to win for communism. Although a change of policy was not to be excluded, this could only come about as a result of 'a sharp change in the situation' – for example, if all channels of entry into the Labour Party were blocked, if the communists were expelled from the unions, or if the communist-controlled unions were to be expelled *en bloc*, or if Britain were engaged in a war.

After the Ninth Congress of the CPGB, where no one raised the question of changing the policy, there took place the Congress of the CPSU, where Bukharin[1] made a ferocious onslaught on the British Labour Party, after which the question of a change of policy was raised with the CPGB by the Comintern representative. The majority of the party leaders did not regard as sound the argument for a change put by the Comintern, hence the thesis quoted above. Yet shortly afterwards the CPGB adopted the Comintern line, and that without the emergence of any of the factors laid down in the central committee's thesis as the necessary preconditions for abandoning its long-established policy in relation to the Labour Party. The immediate question that arises is not: why this complete about-turn by the CPGB? (since we know that it had willy-nilly to accept Comintern policy); nor is it: did the change have a good or a bad effect on the fortunes of the party? It is in fact, what caused the Comintern change of line?

A turn in Russian policy away from a relatively conciliatory course towards a 'sharpening of the class struggle' began to be manifested in 1927. The post-war period of direct revolutionary attack upon world capitalism had, after a transition stage between

1921 and 1923, given way to a policy of 'united front' appeals to the international labour movement, which achieved its high point in the establishment of the Anglo-Russian Committee. This in its turn gave way to a fresh 'class against class' policy against the social-democratic parties in the west. These three phases of Comintern policy – 1) revolutionary offensive; 2) united front retreat; 3) renewed offensive – corresponded to and directly reflected the Russian domestic situation: 1) war communism; 2) the New Economic Policy retreat; 3) forced collectivisation and 'liquidation of the kulaks as a class'.

In the course of his political report to the Fifteenth Congress of the CPSU (bolsheviks)[2] in December 1927, Stalin said:

> The stabilisation of capitalism is becoming increasingly decayed and unstable [sic]. Whereas a year or two ago it was possible, and necessary, to speak of the ebb of the revolutionary tide in Europe, today, we have all the grounds for asserting that *Europe is obviously entering the period of a new revolutionary upswing.*[3]

From this prognosis Stalin concluded that there would inevitably be 'a strengthening of interventionist tendencies in the camp of the imperialists', and that therefore the danger of war against the USSR was 'one of the fundamental factors in the present situation'.[4]

Stalin's evidence for the imminence of war consisted of England's note concerning the financial assistance given by the Russian unions to the coal-miners on strike; the raids upon the Soviet mission in China (Peking, Tientsin, Shanghai); the London police raid on Arcos, the All-Russian Co-operative Society, in May 1927; Great Britain's subsequent rupture of diplomatic relations; the assassination in June 1927 of Volkov (the Soviet envoy in Poland); terrorist acts by British hirelings in the USSR;[5] and strained relations with France on the question of the recall of Rakovsky.[6]

It is a moot point whether the Russian leaders genuinely believed that such incidents demonstrated the existence of a concerted plot by the imperialists to prepare the ground for war against the Soviet Union. What is not in doubt is Stalin's determination to make this the theme of communist agitation in every country. In July 1927 he was arguing that

> It is hardly open to doubt that the chief contemporary question is that of the threat of a new imperialist war. It is not a matter of some indefinite and immaterial 'danger' of a new war. It is a matter of a real and material *threat* of a new war in general, and a war against the USSR in particular.

To make sure that everyone understood what he meant by a 'general war' between unnamed countries and a 'particular' war by other unnamed countries against the USSR, he went on to conclude that 'our' task consisted in 'beating the alarm in all countries in Europe', in 'putting into the stocks all those leaders of the workers' movement who "consider" the threat of a new war an "invention" ', and in 'strengthening our rear and clearing out the rubbish'.[7] In short, the Stalinists were about to launch a war on the home front, against the 'rubbish', i.e. the inner-party Left Opposition and against the peasantry. This was to be justified by the allegedly imminent danger from abroad:

> What can we say after all this of our wretched opposition and its new attacks on the party in face of the threat of a new war? What can we say about the opposition finding it timely, when war threatens, to strengthen the attacks on the party.[8]

This unscrupulous smear tactic was effective since it was axiomatic – even for those who may have thought the war scare an 'invention' – that sooner or later an imperialist war against Russia was inevitable.

The Fifteenth Congress of the CPSU gave the death-blow politically to the Opposition inside the party, expelling members of the Joint Opposition and allowing them to be readmitted only if they recanted. Trotsky, who had been expelled from the party in November 1927, was deported to Alma Ata in Turkestan in January 1928 and excluded from Russia in February 1929. The decisions of this Congress set the course for the super-industrialisation of the country, based upon the forced collectivisation of agriculture, that is, super-exploitation of the peasantry. This entailed semi-military operations to crush the resistance of the peasants and therefore also intensified police action against the defeated Opposition, or, more exactly, against those among them who had not capitulated and were fighting a rearguard action against Stalin, 'the grave-digger of the revolution' in Trotsky's phrase.

The Russian domestic turn to a 'class against class' policy was exported, through the ECCI, to all the communist parties abroad. The programme of 'peaceful co-existence of the two economic systems, the capitalist and the socialist', advanced by the Soviet delegation at the Geneva international economic conference in May 1927, was now no longer valid. From the policy of class collaboration – strikingly exemplified in the communist alliance with Chiang Kai-shek, hailed by Stalin as his 'comrade-in-arms' – there was a violent swing to 'ultra-leftism'.

The keynote of the new policy in Britain was sounded by Stalin when he said, in the speech quoted above :

> Not long ago a protest was received from the well-known leaders of the English labour movement, Lansbury, Maxton, and Brockway, against the shooting of twenty terrorists and incendiarists from among the Russian princes and nobility. I cannot regard these English labour leaders as enemies of the USSR. But they are worse than enemies.[9]

The phrase 'worse than enemies' sums up the attitude now to be adopted by the CPGB towards the British labour leaders.

The change in the CPGB's policy was not unargued. The British party leadership was divided on the issue before the Ninth Plenum of the ECCI which confirmed the new line, with a majority in support of the old line, and a minority against. But the arguments advanced by the majority were rejected in favour of the Dutt – Pollitt minority thesis, submitted to the Ninth Plenum.

The enlarged Ninth Plenum of the ECCI (February 1928) was convened expressly for the purpose of affixing the seal of Comintern approval on the decisions of the Fifteenth Congress of the CPSU, insofar as these directly affected the parties abroad : primarily the measures against the Trotskyist opposition,[10] and secondly, the thesis that Europe 'was obviously entering into the period of a new revolutionary upswing' (Stalin).

The endorsement of the Ninth Plenum resolution on the line to be followed in Britain is described in a statement of the CPGB as follows:

> The Ninth Plenum opened at the beginning of February 1928, and the discussion on the British question which ensued is recorded in the volume, *Communist Tactics in Britain*, which the party has subsequently published. *Scarcely any discussion had taken place on this side, however, when the Plenum resolution became available* [added emphasis], and was immediately published (24 February). Probably owing to the completeness of the change of policy involved, considerable doubt existed in the Political Bureau as to the significance of some of the clauses of the resolution, particularly as even an interim report of the party delegation was not available until 6 March. This doubt was reflected in the party and in a general hesitation to give a definite lead to the party. On 14 March, however, following a full report from the delegation and an exhaustive discussion, the Political Bureau *unanimously* endorsed the new line as a complete change of policy, and a few days later the central committee *unanimously* adopted the same decision.[11]

Although 'scarcely any discussion' had taken place in the party, the directing bodies accepted the new line unanimously; and only after this, as the report later says, was 'An energetic campaign undertaken to explain and popularise the new line, both in the party ... and amongst the workers ...' In other words, the Politburo and the CC (Central Committee) imposed this complete change on the membership, just as the Russian leaders, via the ECCI, had imposed it on them. Yet, as events showed, it was one thing to obtain a unanimous acceptance from the CPGB leadership, and quite another to drill the membership up to the standard required. How this was eventually done will be shown in the next chapter. Let us now consider the discussion at the Ninth Plenum.

A 'British Commission' had been set up to thrash out this matter. Bukharin, replacing Zinoviev as president of the CI, brought all his considerable powers of persuasion, and, even more telling, the weight of his revolutionary prestige, to bear on the British delegates representing the majority view of their central committee. 'We say that the British party must take a sharp turn to the left', he declared.[12] However, in response to the views expressed by the 'majority' British delegates, he appeared ready to make a certain concession. There was a tendency, he said, for the Labour Party to be transformed into a social-democratic party, that is, a party in which the communists would not be permitted to operate. He did not claim that this transformation had already been effected; the process was still incomplete. Consequently he was in favour of continuing the campaign for affiliation to the Labour Party, although it was possible that it might have to be abandoned in the near future. The 'peculiar structure' of this party could be utilised for the time being, without basing any 'great hopes' on the tactic. Thus far Bukharin appeared to support the views held by the British CC 'majority'. But he then proceeded to the question: What were they to do about Labour candidates during elections?

Bukharin argued that such candidates were 'obligatory' on them, although they were not members of the Labour Party but only politically bound by its discipline as members of the trade unions. This fact was of enormous importance for 'our party'. Was it worthwhile to perpetuate this kind of discipline, was it necessary to violate it? 'This is one of the most vital questions of our policy and tactics in Great Britain.' If they submitted to this discipline then they would be pushed aside by the Labour Party and trade-union leaders; they would disappear as an independent party, as a communist party. This discipline had therefore to be broken in the interests of preserving the independence of the party. In effect, Bukharin is here saying that Lenin had been wrong in 1920, when he had argued that the CPGB did not yield one iota of its independence by supporting Labour candidates.

Bukharin recognised that such a course would probably result in the complete banning of communists as trade-union delegates to the Labour Party locally and nationally, but he accepted this as a necessary evil. He did not, however, recognise that it would also make nonsense of any campaign for affiliation to the Labour Party.

The main slogan adopted by the previous congress of the CPGB – the fight for a Labour government – had been erroneous, he said. 'Now the CC admits that it was wrong, it is ready to correct this.' (He did not raise the question of what the membership of the CPGB might think about the matter.) Yet in spite of this admission, 'it wants to put precisely this slogan as the basis of its tactics'. The entire argument against the policy of the ECCI continued to be based on this error. The British comrades persisted in their resistance to the new line; they did not want to 'spoil their relations with the Labour Party'; and 'they put forward as a vital argument that the masses will consider us blacklegs in relation to the Labour Party if we put up our own candidates'. Bukharin brushed this aside with the advice that

> . . . we must explain to the masses why we have changed our tactics. In my opinion it is not only possible but necessary to address the CC [meaning the executive committee] and the local organisations of the Labour Party with a united front proposal, pointing out in it their treachery, etc. by doing which we should show our intention to prevent their amalgamation with the bourgeoisie, and to help them make common cause with other sections of the proletariat.

It is difficult to understand how Bukharin – in the words of Lenin's testament 'the most valuable and biggest theoretician of the party' – could have put the matter so crudely; how he could have been so naive as to imagine that such an approach had the slightest chance of success in the given political circumstances. But there it was. 'We say that the British party must take a sharp turn to the left.' The dilemma facing the *British* communists had really nothing to do with the matter; whatever their misgivings about the new course they were going to be saddled with it. The majority of the leadership indeed viewed the 'left' turn with the gravest apprehension, and the membership, too, as time showed, were far from happy with it. But in the long run it was accepted. In this best disciplined section of the Comintern there was no split on the issue.

It was not accepted without a struggle. Gallacher in particular displayed great reluctance to discard the lesson Lenin had drummed into his head. He refused to agree that the Labour Party was 'a third bourgeois party'; he could not for the life of him see that Lenin's 1920 view had become obsolete. Had he not argued with Lenin on this same problem, pointed out to him 'the treachery of Henderson', 'the betrayal of the miners', and so forth? 'I pointed out that they had exposed themselves to the masses. Never mind, said Lenin, you must keep on with the job.' And if they now went along to the local Labour parties and said that their candidates were 'simply bourgeois candidates, members of a bourgeois party, then the workers would want to know why we apply for affiliation'.[13]

There was really no answer to this, and Bukharin did not try to find one. It would seem that he accepted the retention of the affiliation tactic simply as a sop to the CC majority view, knowing that the new course would in any case make it nonsensical. Maybe he could not understand all the fuss about saying one thing and doing another.

Unlike Bukharin, the Dutt – Pollitt minority did not think there was anything to be gained by concealing the fact that oil and water do not mix. 'It is clear', their minority thesis stated, 'that once the new policy of independent fight is begun, the basis for our campaign for affiliation, which has been of such good service in the past so long as there was scope for it, is finished.'[14] J.T.Murphy was prepared to go even further than just discarding the affiliation campaign. He proposed setting up a rival 'labour party'. Those local Labour parties that had been disaffiliated for communist activity should, he suggested, launch an appeal to the labour rank-and-file to 'organise themselves into a national anti-capitalist party such as was originally conceived the Labour Party to be' (sic).[15] This bold scheme found favour with no one but Murphy.

From the Russian angle, all this was really quite beside the point; the British scene was of concern only insofar as it affected Russia. As Bukharin put it:

Only a few years ago many British trade-union leaders were opposed to the Polish invasion of the USSR. Quite considerable support was then given to the Soviet government. This is a fact. Is such a thing possible now? No, the situation has changed. The objective cause of this change is the change in the international situation. The USSR is now conceived of by the British trade-union leaders and chiefs of the Labour Party no longer as an isolated state embodying the proletarian dictatorship which carried on a struggle against the Polish bourgeois state, but as a force which supports various colonial movements and particularly the Chinese revolution.

What exactly was Bukharin saying? Was it not just that the Russian leaders have lost faith in the revolutionary potential of the western proletariat and have turned their attention elsewhere, to 'various colonial movements'? He went on :

This directly touches the British state and its imperialist interests. This is responsible for the entirely different attitude with regard to the question of war, the question of relations with the USSR and many other international issues because the axis around which all international problems now revolve is the question of relations with the USSR, the colonial question, etc.

Thus everything revolves around the central question of relations with the USSR. Bukharin was simply saying in an involved way what Stalin put bluntly : that Britain was the leading spirit in a projected attack on the USSR.

Turning to 'events of lesser importance', Bukharin argued that sharp conflicts with the reformists were inevitable, because the reformists were opposed to strikes and therefore 'opposed to higher wages and shorter working hours'. On all 'small questions concerning the everyday life of the British proletariat' there would be ranged against the communists the 'gigantic government machine', of which the reformist leaders would be an integral part. He accepted that this situation did not yet exist, but insisted that it was approaching 'at a rapid rate' (the implication being that it could not be prevented). Therefore : 'It would be a mistake and absurd to see in Great Britain . . . only one enemy, the Conservative Party . . . We cannot ignore the existence of the second hostile camp.'

This 'second hostile camp', from being just 'social-democratic' was now on its way to becoming, in Stalin's phrase, 'the twin brother of fascism'; precisely as the Opposition in the Russian party, from being a 'socialist-democratic deviation' became 'fascists', 'intelligence agents of the imperialists'.

J.R.Campbell wound up the discussion on behalf of the central committee of the CPGB with a well-reasoned appeal for retention of the existing tactic. Not wishing to appear any less revolutionary than the Dutt – Pollitt minority, he agreed that 'we have not only one enemy, the capitalist class to fight, but also a second enemy – their lackeys 'within the labour movement'; but he insisted that no sound reasons had been put forward for the proposed turn. Concluding his argument, which demonstrated an understanding of the British political situation much superior to that of Bukharin or of the delegates from Germany, France, Italy and the USA, he said that he did not suppose he had convinced the majority of the commission, although he thought he detected a wavering here and there.

The outcome of the commission's deliberations was a resolution that threw a few sops to the majority and gave the minority all it desired. The affiliation campaign was to be maintained, but 'converted into an offensive fight against the treacherous leadership of the Labour Party'; the slogan of a Labour government had to be replaced by that of a 'Revolutionary Workers' Government'; consequently, the party would put forward the largest possible number of its own candidates and also support candidates of the disaffiliated Labour Party branches in opposition to the Labour Party's 'scab candidates', although in 'some districts active support to Labourites' favouring communist affiliation and supporting 'elementary demands of the working class' would also be permitted.

This resolution was moved by none other than Campbell himself, who now abandoned the position he had so vigorously defended during the discussions. No one had any illusions, he said, about the difficulties that would confront the party in the operation of the new tactic, but the plenum had shown the correct way forward to victory. Gallacher assured those present that 'the members of the British delegation are thoroughly convinced, as a result of the many discussions we have had, that this is the line the party must follow'. Hitherto adamant in his opposition, he now expressed on behalf of the British comrades present his conviction that the party executive would unanimously accept the resolution, that the membership would discuss it thoroughly, and that by the end of the year the party would be stronger than ever.

In the event, the effect of the new line on the fortunes of the CPGB was disastrous. It is true that it did not cause such serious dissension among the leadership as occurred in the continental parties, but it did have the same result – the establishment of a leadership that would in future carry out Comintern policy without reservations of any kind. It also brought disarray in the ranks, a very serious loss in membership, and decline in influence.

6.
Left Turn

The world economic crisis began shortly after the Labour Party took office in 1929. Although the full effects of the crisis were not felt until the beginning of the thirties, the British economy had been experiencing a permanent crisis ever since the end of its relatively brief post-war boom. The register of unemployed in November 1929 already showed a figure of 1,326,000. By January 1930 the figure was 1,520,000; and it rose thereafter as follows: April: 1,761,000; July: 2,070,000; October: 2,319,000; December: 2,500,000; June 1931: 2,707,000. The peak was reached in January 1933 under the National government: 2,955,000. It should be noted that the suffering and misery inflicted on working people was far worse than even these statistics indicate, since they refer only to insured workers, and also since they do not take into account those struck off the register for 'not genuinely seeking work', as the official phrase had it. Unemployment naturally affected many party members themselves; it was less difficult for employers to get rid of militants, and workers were less prepared to take strike action. From the massive total of 162,233,000 in 1926, days lost by strikes fell to a record low of 1,174,000 and 1,388,000 in 1927 and 1928 respectively and in 1929 they reached only 8,287,000. They fell again in 1930 to 4,399,000; and in 1931 and 1932 were only 6,983,000 and 6,488,000 respectively.

Although the 1926 defeat and the growing acuteness of the economic crisis weakened the immediate fighting capacity of the workers in the industrial field, it inevitably made them more receptive to political criticism of the capitalist order. Yet the Communist Party did not gain ground but lost it. In the circumstances, dissatisfaction with the leadership was inevitable among the rank and file. This made it all the easier for the Comintern executive to gain acceptance for its ultra-left line.

The report of the British Commission of the Ninth Plenum of the ECCI (February 1928) opened up a discussion within the CPGB that was to be the last of its kind. Once the issues raised by this report had been finally resolved and a leadership installed that was prepared to carry out the new line to the satisfaction of the ECCI, there would be no more such discussion: all subsequent shifts of a policy would be determined from above, and would – with one speedily corrected exception – always register a strict conformity with the general line of Stalinism.

In an introduction to this report, Campbell wrote that the Central Committee

> underestimated the extent to which the bureaucracy had succeeded in consolidating its influence in the Labour Party and rendering all left-wing work in that body impossible . . . Those of us who stood for the old policy in the discussion are not afraid to admit that we were mistaken, that the development of events has convinced us that we were wrong . . .

That such a lame excuse should be advanced is in itself revealing. No one with the slightest knowledge of the Labour Party needs to be told that the bureaucracy has never been able to suppress the left wing. No matter how many local branches might be disaffiliated, so long as the Labour Party's mass base remained the trade unions there would always be a left wing in some form or other.

So far as the membership of the CPGB was concerned, the new line arose from a re-evaluation of the Labour Party and the unions. It was not apparent to the great majority of members, nor probably to most of the leaders, that for the ECCI all these arguments about the peculiar structure of the British labour movement were beside the point. The left turn was international in scope, part of Stalin's struggle against the men of October, and his destruction of the Left and then of the Right Opposition in Russia. There could be no exceptions to it.

The 'sharpening of the struggle' in Russia put the British party in a difficult situation. Regrettably, the 'broad masses of the working class' could not have been less concerned than they were with the Trotskyist Opposition. On the other hand, they were concerned with the election of a Labour government, to which the party was now strenuously opposed. In the 1929 general election the Labour vote leaped to over eight million, compared with under six million in 1924, and gave the country its second Labour government. The communist candidates, although contesting many more seats, received even fewer votes than in 1924.

The reason for the decline was obvious enough, but any outright opposition to the new line had been effectively squashed. The Tenth Congress of the party in January 1929 had adopted the new line and that was that. This did not mean, however, that the party as a whole had fully grasped what it meant. Failure to appreciate its full import can be seen from the close voting on the question of what was to be done about the National Left-wing Movement, consisting of existing and expelled members of the Labour Party, and headed by Ralph Bond. Should this body be wound up or not? There were 55 votes for shutting up shop and 52 for business as usual. In consequence of this narrow majority the matter was referred back to the Politburo for a re-statement of policy.

The reluctance of the established leadership to go the whole Stalinist hog resulted in a campaign against them by the ECCI (it should be remembered that from 1924 to 1928 no Comintern congress was held).[1] The ECCI's dissatisfaction with the British party leadership led to the calling of the Eleventh Party Congress before the year was up. This 'historic' Leeds congress had before it instructions from the ECCI to set aside all hesitations and vacillations, to put an end once and for all to the bad internal situation of the party, and to prepare for the new 'rising revolutionary tide'. These instructions were published in the *Communist Review* of February 1930. They referred to 'the fascisisation of the Labour Party and its appendage, the sham Lefts (Maxton, Cook, Kirkwood), who play the cowardly and treacherous role of deceiving the workers . . .'; said that, 'The new line demands that the communist parties, while not in the least diminishing their activity in the trade unions, initiate and develop independent organs of struggle . . . for the fight against the employers as well as against the fascist Labour Party and trade-union bureaucracy'; and stressed the pressing need for the party to transfer its main effort to the factories and to develop the Minority Movement into a powerful opposition to the established trade unions. 'The over-estimation of capitalist stabilisation by the party leadership, the inability to see the development of the trade unions and the Labour Party towards social-fascism, the dragging at the tail of the sham Left representatives of social-fascism (Cook and Maxton), hindered the party from realising the necessity for new and independent forms of struggle. The deviation of a number of leading members of the party in this direction explains the resistance to the complete independent action of the Communist Party against the Labour Party, the passive subordination to trade union legality . . . The 'right-wing' leaders of the party must be 'brought out into the open and ruthlessly exposed'.

In preparation for the Leeds Congress, an attack was launched against the existing party leadership through a resolution published in the *Communist Review* in September 1929. This castigated the 'right mistakes committed by the leadership, who interpreted the new line as being mainly a changed electoral tactic'. Further,

> The mistakes and shortcomings of the leadership are all the more glaring in view of the growing critical attitude of the membership, which was first revealed immediately after the Ninth Plenum. The Tenth Party Congress showed clearly a new spirit of awakening among the new membership expressed in the delegates' criticism of the CC's policy. The CC welcomes the strong and healthy spirit of self-criticism of the London, Manchester and Newcastle district party committees . . . The party membership has been in advance of the leadership in appreciating the new situation and desiring the more energetic carrying through of the new line.
>
> This situation shows the necessity of making immediate changes in the leadership, in order to guarantee the carrying out of the Comintern line.
>
> The CC therefore decides to remove three members of the Polit-

buro and Secretariat and to strengthen these organs, especially by drawing in proletarian comrades from the factories. The CC regards these changes as the first steps in the general renewal of the party cadres.

In considering the above, it must be borne in mind that membership had dropped from 7,377 in September 1927 to 3,500 in January 1929. By the time the above resolution was published it had fallen still farther. It is reasonable to assume that this very serious loss of membership was a direct result of the new line. However, the framers of this resolution blamed the leadership for not carrying out the new line with the requisite energy, that is, they simply echoed the criticism of the Comintern officials. These officials – who spoke in the name of an organisation that had in reality ceased to exist, since despite its statutes four years had elapsed between the Fifth and the Sixth World Congress (and another seven would pass before the final, Seventh Congress) – these officials were well aware that strong criticism had been made of the new line, by both rank-and-file members and leading figures. This lack of respect for authority could no more be tolerated in the British party than in the Russian. There had to be installed a leadership 'guaranteed' – as the resolution put it – to carry out the Comintern line without the slightest hesitation.

The decision to change the British party leadership had already been made by the Comintern functionaries before the Leeds Congress and anyone who wanted to retain office had to demonstrate that he would give them no cause for the slightest concern as to his loyalty. The party membership was not aware that the matter had been settled behind the scenes. They were unaware of the ferocity of the Russian inner-party struggle; the verbal and physical thuggery employed by the Stalinists; the use of the GPU against the men of October; the degeneration of the party and the state. If any were perplexed and uneasy about the fall of their heroes of yesterday (of Trotsky, Zinoviev, Bukharin – but the others, who knew their names then?), this led to no deep questioning: the myth was too strong; whatever had happened there, the Revolution remained.

There were those among the leadership, however, and among those aspiring to office, who knew very well that their future in the party depended on gaining the goodwill of Moscow. As Tapsell, who together with Rust was a front man for the Russian '*apparatchikis*' attack on the British leadership, wrote later in the *Communist Review* of July 1930:

> Theoretical training and ability were not the questions upon which the Leeds Congress adopted a change of leadership. Quite correctly, it was made a question of a leadership which would strive to really carry out the line of the Comintern.

One thing was clear, then: it was not the line which was responsible for the disastrous fall in membership and sales of party literature, not the line but the leadership. This conviction was strengthened still further by the welter of accusation and counter-accusation, humble admissions of errors counter-balanced by reference to the no less serious errors of others, as each leader jockeyed for position. Was not the need for a change of leadership all too obvious?

But the Russians were taking no chances. For the first time the Russian 'panel' method of election was used; that is, voting was on a list of recommended candidates drawn up beforehand – an admirable method for ensuring bureaucratic control. Wal Hannington, leader of the National Unemployed Workers Movement committee from 1921, was the only one to challenge this method, secure nomination from the floor, and be elected. Only 12 of the members of the old central committee were elected, and to these 23 new members were added.

The stage was now set for the vigorous application of the new line. One thing only was lacking – a daily newspaper. Bukharin had earlier pointed out that this was essential if the party were to be taken at all seriously as an independent political force. Pollitt – general secretary since August – had then called for a campaign to this end – 'the systematic collection of workers' pennies as a means of making the daily really the workers' own paper.'

Less than a month after the Eleventh Congress a sufficient number of workers' pennies had apparently been collected to make possible the launching of the *Daily Worker*. In view of all the circumstances, this achievement, had it really been a matter of 'workers' pennies', would have been truly remarkable. The pre-congress resolution of the central committee published in the *Communist Review* of September 1929 had recognised that 'the amount of money raised by the party in connection with its various campaigns is grossly inadequate'. After the Eleventh Congress party membership continued to fall and by November 1930 had slumped to 2,555, less than half the membership claimed in 1922.

Here the matter of fund-raising is not simply an organisational problem; it is a political question. Pollitt's 'workers' pennies' was not a figure of speech; he was recalling Lenin's words when, back in 1921, he had advised Thomas Bell on the subject of founding a workers' paper. Such a paper, Lenin wrote, should not be started 'as a business, not with [a] big sum of money', but as a paper relying solely on the support of the workers. He was of course not referring to a national daily, which would require a large sum of money. In view of the support then being given by the South Wales miners to the Communist International, he suggested that a modest beginning might be made in that district.

> If the communist party of this district cannot collect few £ in order to publish small *leaflets* DAILY as a beginning of the really *proletarian* communist newspaper – if it so, if *every* miner will not pay a penny for it, then there is *not serious*, not genuine affiliation to the III. Int.

(Lenin appeared to be somewhat sceptical about this affiliation vote, for he had earlier in the same letter asked: 'how much miners were *really* represented in Cardiff 24/VIII 1921?'). He advised that 'the paper must be *not too revolutionary* in the beginning', in order to avoid suppression by the government:

> If you will have three editors, at least one must be *non-communist* (at least two genuine workers). If 9/10 of the workers do not buy this paper, if 2/3 workers ... do not pay special contributions (f.i. 1 penny *weekly*) for THEIR paper – it will be no workers' newspaper.[2]

For Lenin all organisational problems had to be considered from the viewpoint of revolutionary politics. Organisational methods had to be consonant with, and be an expression of the political philosophy of, the movement. There could be a genuine workers' daily, expressing the unity of the vanguard and the miners, only if the miners themselves made it possible, with their pennies, by their participation.

Pollitt culled the phrase 'workers' pennies' from this letter, but the launching of the *Daily Worker* was not the modest beginning of which Lenin wrote and in view of the general decline of support by the workers could not have been possible without outside financial aid.

The more rabid defenders of the capitalist social system, with plenty of cash at their disposal and no great scruples as to how they used it, made the most of the evidence showing that the CPGB was heavily dependent on financial aid from Moscow. No doubt this play on nationalist prejudices had its effect on backward elements among the workers, but it can hardly have cut much ice with militant trade unionists. The principle of international fraternal aid requires no defence. Yet in the matter of subsidies for the actual running expenses of a party, everything depends upon the spirit in which they are given and accepted. But by then the Russian party had, through the so-called Lenin enrolment, already been swamped with careerists eager for the fleshpots of power. For these people, who would be used to hound the men of October into prison, exile and death, the ideals of communism meant less than nothing. They embodied all the worst traits of the Russian peasantry – acquisitiveness, brutality, anti-semitism, hatred of intellectuals, parochialism. What importance did international solidarity have for them? At best, a shibboleth void of meaning. The spirit imbuing the Soviet government's decree of 1917 on aid to the international revolutionary movement[3] was totally alien to them. For the men of the Stalinist machine aid had become a simple matter of cash paid out for services rendered or to be rendered.

There can be no question that those responsible for running

the party organisation in this and other countries were to some degree or other influenced by the subsidies given by the Comintern. Between 5 July 1927 and 20 April 1928 the CPGB received the sum of £27,998.[4] This at a time when, as has been noted above, the central committee was complaining of the 'grossly inadequate' amount of money raised by the party members themselves. Even if one assumes that all those in the party who were in the know were quite uninfluenced in their views – an assumption not easy to accept – such an imbalance between subsidies and 'workers' pennies' must be recognised as unhealthy in any circumstances.

The rank and file of the CPGB did not see the danger in these subsidies. They were not privy to the manoeuvres and intrigues going on behind the scenes. They knew nothing of Stalinist take-over in Russia. For them the vision of the Russian Revolution remained untarnished.[5]

The first issue of the *Daily Worker* carried greetings from the presidium of the ECCI in Moscow, which ran, in part:

> It will be the rallying point for the fight ... against the Labour government of rationalisation, anti-Soviet intrigues, colonial brutalities and preparation for another imperialist war. The *Daily Worker* must expose the reactionary schemes of the trade-union bureaucracy, and the deceptions of the Labourites and the pseudo-Lefts.

The first editor of the *Daily Worker* was William Rust, the CPGB representative on the ECCI, the front man for the Russian functionaries' attack on the old leadership of the CPGB.

7.
The 'Third Period'

The Sixth World Congress of the Comintern met in 1928 (July – September) to rubber-stamp the views and opinions arrived at by the secretariat of the CPSU. This was the last congress presided over by one of the great figures of the Russian Revolution, Nikolai Bukharin. Just over 62 per cent of the delegates were party officials. The programme of the Comintern, which had been drafted by Bukharin (who, let it be recalled, would be shot as a 'traitor' ten years later) and discussed before at great length by numerous meetings of functionaries, was adopted at this congress. The cornerstone of the programme was the Stalinist theory of 'socialism in one country'. Trotsky's criticism of this programme was not made available to the delegates, although a few of them came into possession of an abridged version.[1]

It was at this congress that the so-called 'third period' of capitalism was proclaimed. Having passed through two post-war phases – revolutionary upheaval and temporary stabilisation – capitalism was now in a phase of a relative economic stabilisation resulting from rationalisation, with a sharpening of internal and international antagonisms, and a consequent 'revolutionary upswing'. This revolutionary upswing, forecast by Stalin in 1927, would reveal its full scope with the inevitable onset of the world economic crisis.

In 1929 world capitalism did indeed pass into a phase of acute crisis and there was indeed a potentially revolutionary situation. In October the US stock market collapsed, leading to a failure of banks and rapidly rising unemployment. This led to a period of slump and mass unemployment in the US and throughout Europe. As we shall see, however, the regimentation imposed on the communist parties in the interests of 'socialism in one country' made them incapable of anything other than carrying out orders, orders that everywhere smoothed the path for reaction.

The Eleventh Congress of the CPGB had finally and permanently resolved the question of the leadership. Henceforth there would not again be even the restricted discussion by the ranks that had taken place before this congress. Instead of policy discussion there would be 'self-criticism', that is to say, criticism of administrative weaknesses, of inefficiency, of failure to apply the line with the requisite energy or adroitness, of the 'shortcomings' of individuals, their 'deviations', and so on.

An official statement of the new attitude towards inner-party criticism was given in the *Communist Review* of June 1931, where it was explained:

> Freedom of criticism is a natural rule of party life. How can the members of the party fail to criticise the party bureau or committee if its work is poor, if it makes mistakes, etc? Without criticism there can be no party. There is no need of speaking of such criticism; it is necessary, it has always been allowed, and always will be. But the party members must be warned against the special slogan of 'free criticism'.

Thus the bounds within which criticism will be 'allowed' are defined. And what is this 'free criticism' against which the members must be warned?

> Whenever the question of criticism is raised the workers [sic] must be careful to see what sort of criticism is being proposed: whether the kind that helps the party to strengthen its foundations or the one which leads to petty-bourgeois views filtering themselves into the party.

From this it would appear that 'free criticism' is nothing other than 'petty-bourgeois criticism'. And what precisely is that? The statement seems to leave it to 'the workers' to decide the meaning. But, even granting the somewhat far-fetched assumption that the workers know what 'petty-bourgeois' views are, what grounds are there for assuming that they are prepared to stand guard over the ideological purity of a party for which they do not display any great urge even to vote? And by what means are they to exercise this control over party discussion? This is nonsense; but nonsense with a purpose. Criticism of policy does not have to be countered by a reasoned argument, it just has to be labelled 'petty-bourgeois' and that's that. 'The workers' are brought in to disguise the fact that someone has to stick on the label and that that someone will be the leadership.

Suppression of discussion within the CPGB was made all the easier for the new leadership since this party had never been notable for a preoccupation with political theory. That is not to say that, in spite of the anti-intellectual bias of the party, no one ever felt the need for political discussion. An illuminating description of the average communist 'local' was given by a Wigan comrade in *The Communist* of December 1928:

> The continued exit of members from our party cannot be explained by a vague reference to 'objective conditions' or even to 'wrong approach' ... The main cause, in my opinion, lies in the *political lifelessness* in our party locals. The average local party committee does not function as the political leadership of the local. It is a purely organisational committee passing on instructions from higher organs and distributing routine tasks of a local character.
>
> Life in the average local becomes an endless routine grind. Work is carried on in grooves and ruts. The relationship between comrades is not built on theoretical discussion and the mutual consciousness of the political aims of the tasks in hand. It is a personal relationship based on routine work and the allocation of funds. In this atmosphere personal friction is easily engendered in which politics do not enter ...
>
> When an attempt is made to raise a discussion on the politics of the task in hand this is discouraged on the grounds of lack of time, or that it is action we need, not talk. The 'practical' chairman of the LPC [Local Party Committee] is intolerant of 'talkers'. It smacks of intellectualism. What are needed are workers ... The test of communist competence becomes chalking pavements and selling the party organ.

It could hardly have been put better.

The Eleventh Congress having, as it were, cleared the decks for action, the tasks of the party were summarised as follows:

to place itself at the head of the rising wave of struggle. To no longer trail behind events, but to march at their head. To assist the workers to break through the shackles of the bureaucratic machine by effective revolutionary leadership. To develop and initiate the strike movement, to link the struggle of the workers with those of the colonies. To understand that every class mass action is part of the struggle against war – the attack on the Soviet Union, which is the pivot of capitalist policy; while the sum of all this is the fight for the overthrow of the Labour government.[2]

The general election of May 1929 had demonstrated the complete indifference of the workers to the appeals of the CPGB. Dutt had informed them that the Labour Party was 'an integral part of the capitalist state' and Pollitt had warned them that it was impossible for any class-conscious worker to vote Labour : 'The fight now in every sphere of political activity, whether in elections, strikes, lock-outs, unemployed demonstrations, etc., is against the enemies, the capitalist class and the Labour Party and the TUC.'[3] This crude, unrealistic assessment of the political situation served only to repel the workers.

The Labour government that resulted from the election resumed diplomatic relations with the USSR in October and a trade agreement was signed in April 1930, but this in no way softened communist hostility. The Tenth Plenum of the ECCI (June 1929), presided over by Molotov, had laid it down that the Labour government would 'conduct an aggressive imperialist policy of war, primarily against the USSR, camouflaging this policy with pacifist phraseology'.[4] If the Labour government had refused to resume diplomatic relations with Russia, this would have been triumphantly adduced as confirmation of the ECCI's outlook. That it did not so refuse, but on the contrary reversed the Tory government's policy in this respect, was of no consequence. Facts that went to throw doubt on the correctness of the line were brushed aside or simply ignored. No question of principle was involved; the line could be, and would be, changed to its opposite in the interests of Russian diplomacy.

In the general election of 1931 the party again campaigned against the Labour Party, obtaining a total of 74,824 votes for its

26 candidates. This was a very poor return indeed for the strenuous efforts of the small band of communists. Why had the workers failed so signally to respond to their propaganda? The country was in the throes of an economic crisis. There were two and a half million unemployed. The Labour government brought to office by the 1929 election, anxious to demonstrate its capacity to govern in a responsible manner, had put its best minds to the task of squaring the capitalist circle. It had finally accepted a Liberal Party motion to set up a committee to discover ways of cutting down government expenditure, in order to 'save the pound'. It was agreed on all sides that the masses were eating too much for the health of the economy. In this respect, the unemployed were felt to be particularly voracious, although no one cared to put it that bluntly. However, the key question was: how much was too much? The cuts recommended by the government May Committee turned out to be too severe for the majority of Labour MPs to stomach. Apart from humanitarian sentiments that may have influenced some (the ILP MPs were of course resolutely opposed to any cuts at all), they all knew full well that acceptance of the May Committee report meant their political death.

The Cabinet was divided and Ramsay MacDonald announced that a 'National' government had been formed, with himself at its head. MacDonald, lion of the Tory drawing-rooms, admired, honoured and respected leader of Labour, had pushed his political philosophy to its logical conclusion. At a time of acute crisis of capitalism the only salvation was 'national unity', everyone pulling together, everyone making sacrifices.

Only two Cabinet ministers followed MacDonald, Snowden and Thomas.[5] The Labour Party as a whole was shocked to the core. MacDonald was a traitor to the labour movement. Bitterly resentful, the Labour Party found itself fighting the 1931 general election not only against the Tories and the Liberals, but also against the National Labour turncoats, and the Communist Party.

The Labour Party dropped two million votes and suffered, from the parliamentary viewpoint, a disastrous defeat. But the hard core of its working-class supporters stood firm. They saw the issue as a class battle. They did not listen to the Communist Party's harangues about the 'social-fascist' Labour Party, about its 'integration with the capitalist state'. Or if they listened, they shrugged their shoulders and turned away. If the party wanted to be listened to, it had to find common ground with them, which in the circumstances of the time could only be found by giving critical support to the Labour Party, since this was where the class feeling of the workers found political expression. Mere denunciation of all reformist leaders, right, left and centre, taught the workers nothing and served only to antagonise them. A campaign of patient, persistent and consistent *explanation* was required; explanation that generalised the day-by-day defensive battles, bringing understanding of capitalism as a *system* and the utter futility of the reformist method of attempting to prettify this or that 'ugly' face of it.

The party's 'isolation . . . from the masses of the workers'[6] can be seen from the membership figures given in the *Communist Review* of August 1932:

Date	Membership
1922	5,116
1926	10,800
1927	7,377
1929 (January)	3,500
1929 (December)	3,200
1930 (May)	2,850
1930 (November)	2,555
1931 (November)	6,279
1932	9,000

Thus, by November 1930 the membership was half that of 1922, shortly after the party's founding. The world crisis stopped the rot, but the improvement was by no means commensurate with the objectively favourable situation. Apart from the fact that a considerable number of the new members were unemployed, it was also admitted that the 1932 figures were to some extent optimistic, since roughly two thirds consisted of 'paper' members. The year 1932 showed therefore little if any progress over 1931. A further weakness was the chronic fluctuation in membership. A fifth of the membership lapsed 'even in those years when the total membership was almost stagnant', the *Communist Review* commented. Further, even after the rise of 1931 the 'social composition' of the party remained unsatisfactory, nearly fifty per cent consisting of unemployed persons and housewives, those without direct association with industry. It seemed that the party had indeed become, in Trotsky's phrase, 'a political thoroughfare' through which people passed on their way elsewhere.

There was one bright area of party activity – the coalminers. Yet even here the adventurist policy thrust upon the party lost it the co-operation of one of its notable supporters, A.J.Cook. To some a mere demagogue, to that dry stick, Beatrice Webb, an 'inspired idiot', Cook was an agitational speaker of extraordinary power, greatly loved by the miners : he was their voice crying out for justice, rousing the generous-hearted to fellow feeling, solidarity; rallying the ranks and sounding the battle-cry of freedom.

Cook's long-standing co-operation with the communists was ended by their switch to ultra-leftism. Before the Tenth Congress they had supported the Cook – Maxton 'socialist revival' campaign when Cook and the ILP leader issued a manifesto saying that the Labour Party had made a 'serious departure from the principles and policy which animated the founders'. Indeed, at one time the Communists claimed the credit for its launching. The campaign was a praiseworthy effort to raise morale and to combat the class-collaboration policy initiated by Sir Alfred Mond (head of ICI) and embraced by the TUC. It did much to strengthen the Labour Party left, in particular the ILP. Resistance to making a clean break with Cook and Maxton had been one of the ECCI's charges against the old leadership of the party; support for their campaign was pointed to as evidence of 'right-deviationism'. The ECCI of course conveniently forgot about its own brand of right deviation – the Anglo-Russian Committee. Now Stalin had decreed that even Cook and Maxton were 'worse than enemies'.

It was particularly hard for the CPGB to look upon Cook as worse than an enemy. True they had criticised him after the general strike, but mildly. It took some time for the break to come.

The policy of 'strengthening the revolutionary trade unions' could, since none such existed in Britain, only mean efforts to create breakaway unions. And here the only significant progress made was among the coal-miners of Scotland.[7]

The CPGB set up the United Mineworkers of Scotland in April 1929, after a long and bitter struggle with the established trade-union bureaucracy, involving a complex series of procedural manoeuvres on both sides. The bureaucracy used every trick of the trade to deny the communists gains they had won by the votes of the union members. Cook himself raised his voice in denunciation of the bureaucrats' tactics, which at one stage led to the bureaucracy itself setting up what was virtually a breakaway union. In the end, however, it was the CPGB that, pressured by the demands of the Comintern line, appeared as the 'splitters' when they announced the formation of the United Mineworkers of Scotland.

This protracted struggle to capture union power involved considerably less than half of the total workforce, 55,000 of whom were then unorganised. Moreover, it brought no recruits to the party, the membership of which dropped – as has already been noted – from 3,500 in January 1929 to 2,850 in May 1930.

For Cook the formation of this union was the final confirmation of his belief that the party was no longer in the workers' camp. He had already made it clear that he was 'opposed to all those who stand in the way' of the achievement of a Labour government[8] and at the same time signed a Miners' Federation statement strongly condemning the CPGB and Minority Movement tactics in the various coalfields, particularly in Scotland (some four months earlier he had refused to sign a similar statement).

Cook gave his reasons for breaking with the communists in the June issue of *Labour Monthly*. Their tactics, he wrote, were to 'continually attack all leaders not members of the CP, since, it is claimed, they are the only pure, the only perfectly honest brand when they possess the CP label'. The party's present tactics were aimed at smashing the Miners' Federation of Great Britain, the TUC, and the Labour Party. 'Comradeship means something higher and nobler than the example set by the British Communist Party in their campaign of personalities, hate, vilification, and destruction.' One might gather from this that it was as much, if not more, the party's style (personalities, hate, vilification) that repelled him, as its actual policy. And sticking to this style, Dutt said 'farewell to him [Cook] without regret and with the contempt that he deserves'. Not one hint of the service Cook had rendered the workers. Only a slanderous amalgam of 'Messrs Cook and the *Daily Mail*'; a distortion of Cook's attack on the party's ethics to an attack on 'the communists and revolutionaries', and a twisting of his argument that trade-union leaders were such through the democratic choice of the rank and file into 'blaming the workers'.

The policy of 'strengthening the revolutionary trade unions' also brought opposition from one of the party's foremost members among trade-union officials, Arthur Horner. Horner's opposition, which came fully into the open only at the beginning of 1931, was purely tactical and did not affect his loyalty to the party as such. In this conflict with the party bureaucracy, he appealed for support to 'a friend in Moscow' (as the Politburo put it, for some reason not wishing to mention Lozovsky[9] by name). He charged that the party had 'disregarded' the South Wales Miners' Federation, and had set up in opposition to the miners' lodges 'artificial' strike committees, which were in fact Minority Movement groups without 'mass contact'. The Politburo counter-charged that Horner was attacking the entire policy of 'independent leadership'. In a very long statement (27 February), published in the *Communist Review* of April 1931, the Politburo referred to the need to 'crush once and for all the remnants of the old leadership, who continue an obstinate struggle against the line of independent revolutionary leadership of the working class by the Communist Party'; accused Horner of placing 'his faith in the social-fascists' bureaucracy and their trade union apparatus', and of being both cowardly in face of the bureaucracy and 'anarchistic' in regard to communist discipline. He had also made 'an open challenge' to the RILU in refusing to attend a meeting of the secretariat of the Miners' International Committee on 14 February. This statement was endorsed by the party central committee. In the course of a reply to further discussion in the following issue of the *Communist Review*, the Politburo argued that South Wales had at one time been the best district in the country so far as contact with the miners was concerned; but it had been

> a formal contact, which breathed belief in the union, which sought changes only within the apparatus of the Federation, that could not see that the big political changes taking place within the whole labour movement called for an entirely new approach to the question of work within the unions.

The logical conclusion of the Russian-inspired policy – the setting up of 'red' unions – is here hinted at pretty broadly, but the party bureaucracy was chary of saying this in so many words. The big difficulty was how to reconcile the new policy with continued work in the established unions for the purpose of their 'capture', which carried with it the danger of 'breathing belief' in them. Horner felt that he could appeal to Moscow precisely because of the equivocal attitude of the ECCI on this tactical problem. While all the emphasis was on setting up communist-controlled bodies based on the place of work and on strike committees, which aimed at replacing the unions, it was at the same time still considered necessary to work within these unions in order to 'capture the trade-union masses'. The ECCI had laid it down at its Tenth Plenum that

> The present period confronts the Comintern with the policy, not of quitting the reformist trade unions or of artificially creating new trade unions, but of carrying on a fight for winning the majority of the working class, in the reformist unions as well as in organisations based upon wider masses (committees of action, factory councils) which pursue the same aims as the revolutionary trade-union movement, but to do so in their own special way.[10]

But at the same time it was argued that communists could

not be opposed on principle to splitting the trade unions. The resolution of the Second Congress of the Comintern had pointed out the conditions under which communists are bound to work for a split, namely: 'Communists should not shrink from splitting the trade-union organisations if to avoid a split would mean to give up revolutionary work in the unions . . .'[11]

From this both sides of the argument could find support. However, general communist propaganda was in harmony with the splitting tactic and frustrated those who, like Horner, were working in the unions to 'capture the masses'. In this dispute the element of personal rivalry was not altogether absent.

The central committee of the party felt it necessary to put its attitude towards this matter on record in a resolution of December 1931, the essential part of which read:

> The line of the 'Left' reformists is simply to win the strike as an end in itself, and where the Right reformists are still in the leadership to prove that the 'Left' proposals for carrying on the strike were the best. The line of the revolutionary opposition, while striving to the utmost to defeat the capitalists and win the strike, has also another object: strengthening the independent fight of the working class and revolutionising the working masses. The strike as an end in itself diverts the attention of the workers from the necessity of continuous struggle against the mineowners and their allies the bureaucracy and from the end of the independent leadership and organisation for this struggle.

Of course there is always the problem of how to combine support for a given strike, necessarily reformist in its immediate objectives, with revolutionary propaganda which has to make it clear to the workers that 'it is not the lowness of wages which forms the fundamental evil, but the wages system itself'.[12] The danger of falling into the error of making the strike an 'end in itself' is ever present and there is little evidence to support the claim by the central committee that they were immune from it. To speak as they did of 'continuous struggle against the bureaucracy' and of 'independent leadership and organisation for this struggle', did not make them any less reformist than the 'Left reformist' Horner, or his close personal friend, Cook, now characterised at the Tenth

Plenum of the ECCI as one of those who formed 'an active and constituent part . . . of social fascism'. Indeed, Comintern pressure, put on the CPGB to demonstrate its effectiveness in carrying out the 'third period' policy, tended precisely to encourage action for the sake of action.

The Eleventh Plenum of the ECCI (March – April 1931) devoted some time to a consideration of the failings of the British party, which was accused of underestimating the speed at which the workers were moving to the left. There had been, said the ECCI, a number of strikes 'not prepared by' the communist party, such as those in Lancashire and South Wales. Moreover, the required shift of emphasis from trade-union branch activity to the creation of factory cells and factory committees had not been made. In this respect the CPGB was in an even worse position than the party in Czechoslovakia and the USA, where a mere 14 per cent and 10 per cent respectively were organised in factory cells. The CPGB was 'one of the weakest spots of the Comintern'. In May 1931 the central committee of the CPGB noted this criticism and called upon the members to raise themselves to the height of the favourable situation then prevailing. They must 'demonstrate before the masses that the reformists were carrying out a policy of social fascism' and that the Labour government, 'far from being the lesser evil . . . is the most effective instrument for attacking the working class at the present time'.

The central theme of the Eleventh Plenum was the danger of war against the USSR, now imminent as a consequence of the triumph of socialism in the USSR and the disintegration of capitalism. Undeterred by the fall of the Labour government, the party pressed on with its onslaught against the Labour Party. A central committee resolution of December 1931, discussing how best to destroy the 'leadership and influence of the Labour Party', emphasised the need to study and put into practice Manuilsky's advice at the Eleventh Plenum. Manuilsky[13] had there complained that many communist parties had not shown the masses clearly and concretely why social democracy was not the 'lesser evil'; that it was not 'worse' than, or 'just as bad as' the fascists, but the main obstacle to the mobilisation of the masses against the dictatorship of the bourgeoisie, because it was the main social support of the bourgeoisie. Signs of deviation from this line had shown themselves in the British party:

> The move towards pacts with the ILP[14] (often under such forms as requests to ILP leaders to head demonstrations, etc., workers' candidates instead of communist candidates, leading fractions of the NUWM [National Unemployed Workers' Movement] acting contrary to the line of the party (in relation to Maxton, etc.) is a sign of opportunist tendencies in the party, revealing themselves in the central committee.
>
> Particularly dangerous deviations were made by the party in the struggle against the ILP which is an inseparable part of British social-fascism. The ILP with the support of the bourgeoisie is the most dangerous barrier between the party and the masses who are becoming radical.[15]

One decision singled out for particular mention was that of allowing the unemployed delegation (accorded an interview by MacDonald in September 1931) to 'get into the hands of Maxton and Kirkwood'. In other words, the NUWM (ostensibly a non-party body) was the communists' baby – hands off![16]

The central committee resolution of January 1932 did not deal only with the failure to handle correctly the unemployed movement; it also summarised the findings of a special commission set up to discover exactly why the party had failed to prosper as it should have prospered in the circumstances of mass unemployment and a discontent so general and profound as to provoke a 'mutiny' even in the British navy.[17]

This commission's investigation was necessarily limited in scope, since there could be no question of reconsidering policy in the light of the actual relationship of forces and the real mood of the workers. All the 'facts' had already been established and the policy laid down by the ECCI. The commission had therefore to attribute the party's evident failure to incorrect application of the line. All shortcomings were consequently ascribed to the inadequacies of individuals and to organisational weaknesses. The remedy allegedly lay in the strict adherence to the ECCI instructions and redoubled energy in their application. There must be 'IRRECONCILABLE STRUGGLE against the Labour Party and the TUC leaders and particularly against the ILP'. The party must 'fasten on all the countless conflicts of a minor and major character arising daily with the employers, foremen, and trade-union bureaucrats . . .' There was no possibility here of facing the fact that unemployment had not induced an attacking spirit among the workers in the industrial field; that there was no rising revolutionary tide.

The rank and file of the British party were pitiably few for the multiplicity of tasks assigned to them. Constantly exhorted by their drill sergeants, themselves harassed by a 'general staff' abroad, the membership was strained to the point of exhaustion. On top of everything else, the mandarins of the ECCI had now laid down international 'days of struggle' on which the various parties were supposed to 'bring the workers on to the street', willy-nilly. Thus 5 March was set apart as a day of international demonstrations against unemployment. In regard to this, an editorial in the *Communist Review* of March 1930, after admitting that the members 'rushed distractedly from one task and one problem to another', gave the North London local a dressing-down for questioning the feasibility of executing this particular order. Yet there was no organisation with a more dedicated rank and file than the CPGB's. The failure to make headway was certainly not due to any lack of energy or self-sacrifice on their part.

An amusing illustration of the state of the party during this period occurs in an article by J.T.Murphy in the *Communist Review* of June 1930, where he wrote that

> In the preparations for March 6, the Manchester Working Bureau put forward, among other proposals, that a number of leading comrades should call on the soldiers in uniform to demonstrate with the workers in the streets. Now, no member of our Party will question the desirability of propaganda among the troops. But when it is realised that in Burnley we had not a single party cell in the mills, that the whole party membership in Burnley did not muster a dozen members, that there had not been the slightest preparation for mass action of the workers, no preliminary work amongst the

soldiers, indeed, that *there are no Burnley barracks and no soldiers* in Burnley, then the absolutely unreal and romantic line of approach by the Bureau can be seen at a glance.

The net result of Stalin's 'class against class' line in Britain was put by Hutt like this : 'Sectarianism had been rife in the application of the "new line" and as a result Communists found themselves in a weaker position in the trade unions and among the organised workers in general than they had been before.'[18] Not the line itself was at fault, only its misapplication. However, one searches in vain through all the mass of party literature for an explanation of how it might have been correctly applied. The plain fact of the matter is that the line itself was 'sectarian'. But even to hint at this would have been to cast doubt on the wisdom of the Soviet leaders. To have really probed into the problem would have been to reveal that they had misread the entire political situation in the most blockheaded manner possible; and that, even worse, they had subordinated all the communist parties to themselves, used them in the interests of their own power struggle in Russia, in the interests of Socialism in One Country, masquerading under the guise of internationalism.

In Britain the influence of the Russian line was baleful. In Germany, it was catastrophic and led directly to Hitler's conquest of power. It was only then, and after some hesitation, that the Russians changed course. They quickly summoned the Comintern from the obscurity into which Stalin had thrust it, to rubber-stamp a complete reversal of the 'third period' policy. A trumpet call was sounded for a 'Popular Front' against fascism. A Popular Front embracing not only the erstwhile social-fascists (an epithet now to be forever expunged from the communists' vocabulary) but all and sundry, everyone and anyone pledged to 'make a stand' against the 'main enemy', now accepted as fascism, in particular its German form, nazism.

The events leading up to this right-about-turn and the manner in which it affected the CPGB will now be examined.

8.
Unity at Any Price

Stalin foreshadowed the possibility of a change of policy on the part of the Soviet Union in an interview with Walter Duranty, of the *New York Times*, in December 1933. 'It is not impossible,' he said, 'that we shall support the League [of Nations], notwithstanding its colossal defects'.[1] Later statements by Litvinov and Molotov also hinted at the same possibility, although less directly. The change of tune was clearly connected with events in Germany and her withdrawal from the League; but the belief that the nazi triumph in January 1933 brought about an immediate radical change in Soviet policy is not borne out by the facts. For at the same time as Stalin was tentatively exploring the chances of a rapprochement with the 'non-aggressive' capitalist states, he was also not neglecting the possibility of coming to an understanding with nazi Germany. The following remarks by Litvinov, made in the course of a speech to the Central Executive Committee of the Supreme Soviet on 29 December 1933, were obvious kite-flying:

> We understand very well the difference between doctrine and policy. It does happen that an opposition, on coming to power, tries to forget the slogans which it used in the fight against its political opponents.
>
> Of course, we have our own opinion about the German regime, and of course we sympathise with the sufferings of our German comrades, but we as marxists are the last who can be reproached with allowing sentiment to prevail over policy. The entire world knows that we can and do maintain relations with capitalist states whatever their regime, even if it is fascist . . . our relations with Germany are determined not by its internal but its external policy.[2]

Could one ask for a better example of utterly shameless cynicism and total lack of principle than this? Soviet diplomacy was obviously vacillating between two possible policies: alliance with the 'have-not' powers or with the 'haves', extension of the 1926 pact of neutrality and friendship with Germany (prolonged in 1931, and the prolongation ratified in May 1933 a few weeks after Hitler's victory) or a defensive – offensive agreement with England and France. In these circumstances, the Comintern functionaries had no instructions to change course.

The Thirteenth Plenum of the ECCI met in Moscow in December 1933. The decisions of this plenum were presented to the CPGB in a report by Pollitt, published as a pamphlet: *Towards Soviet Power*. The title itself shows that the revolutionary phrasemongers were still busy mongering. Pollitt wrote that

> we can see that the crisis of the Second International is a fact. But in the speeches at the plenum [Pollitt had been present], much criticism had been levelled against all the communist parties for their neglect in not being able to take advantage of the position, and more effectively to unmask social democracy before the eyes of the masses who still believe in it, and win them to the Communist Party.

Endorsing the ECCI's view that the communist party of Germany had not been crushed, but, on the contrary, was 'daily strengthening its work'; and that Hitler's victory, by destroying illusions about parliamentary democracy, was assisting the revolutionary forces, Pollitt argued: 'In this way an important weakening of Social Democracy takes place, which, because it is the chief social support of capitalism, leads to a strengthening of the revolutionary forces making for the overthrow of capitalism.' There was apparently no inkling of the fact that the order to about-face would shortly be given. In February 1934 the agit-prop department was still saying: 'We must also give attention to social-fascism, and be able to show the role of British labour in the drive to fascism' (*Communist Review*). In June 1934 Palme Dutt was still in all seriousness arguing that 'The line of Lansbury is the line of fascism' (*Labour Monthly*); and as late as February 1935 he was writing in the same journal: 'A Labour government, any Labour government. . . . means first and above all the tying of the workers to capitalism, the throttling of the workers' struggle, the carrying through of the capitalist offensive against the workers and the colonial peoples . . .' The rise of fascism, genuine fascism, had taught him nothing.

Yet even as the party officials clung obstinately to the old line a new course was in process of formation. For a whole year Stalin had made no pronouncement whatever on the subject of Hitler's accession to power. Then, at the Seventecnth Congress of the Russian party in January 1934, he touched on this matter in terms similar to those employed earlier by Litvinov:

> Of course, we are far from being enthusiastic about the fascist regime in Germany. But fascism is not the issue here, if only for the reason that fascism in Italy, for instance, has not prevented the USSR from establishing the best relations with that country.[3]

With fascist Italy the 'best relations' had been established; why not also with nazi Germany? On the other hand, there were the pacts of non-aggression with Poland and France, with whom relations in the past had been 'not at all good'. German politicians, said Stalin, had seen this as 'an orientation towards France and Poland', a switch from opposition to support of the Versailles treaty. 'That was not true', said Stalin. The USSR had never had, and had not then, any 'orientation' towards Poland, France, Germany or any other country. 'Our orientation in the past and our orientation at the present time is towards the USSR, and towards the USSR alone'.[4] In short, we are ready, in the interests of socialism in one country, to establish 'the best of relations' with no matter what country, what regime.

Nazi Germany was also playing its own game, in the interests of its own brand of national socialism. Stalin's broad hint was noted, but Hitler made no move. So, in March Anthony Eden was feted at the Kremlin, in September the Soviet Union joined the League of Nations, that 'den of robbers' (Lenin), and in August 1935 the Seventh World Congress of the Communist International was convened to launch the policy of the 'People's Front'.

The Bulgarian party leader Georgi Dimitrov,[5] replacing

Manuilsky as general secretary of the CI secretariat, was put up to proclaim the new policy. He was concerned to defend the new policy as in no way a departure from the old; since it was so evidently a departure, his speech was an odd mixture of revolutionary phrasemongering and admonitions that precisely such idle chatter must in future be rigorously eschewed. The following extract from his speech may be cited as an illustration of his approach:

> Comrade Dutt was right in his contention that there has been a tendency among us to contemplate fascism in general ... erroneously classifying all reactionary measures of the bourgeoisie as fascism and going as far as calling the entire non-communist camp fascist. The struggle against fascism was not strengthened but rather weakened in consequence.[6]

Thus the whole 'third period' policy became 'a tendency among us' – just a 'tendency', nothing more. The fact that Dutt, the ideological mentor of the British party, had done his full share in fostering this 'tendency', together with all the other party leaders in all the other countries, was studiously ignored. Immediately after making this point, Dimitrov went on to rap the knuckles of those comrades who regarded Roosevelt's 'New Deal'[7] as 'an even clearer and more pronounced form of the development of the bourgeoisie towards fascism than the "National government" in Great Britain',[8] and to argue that the rise of fascism and the resultant changed situation 'has made it increasingly difficult, and in some countries actually impossible, for social democracy to preserve its former role of bulwark of the bourgeoisie'.[9]

The Seventh World Congress had been convened not to survey the results of the 'third period' policy, but to proclaim with all possible ballyhoo that there was a 'changed political situation' which required not simply a united front of the reformists and the communists but a 'united people's front in the struggle for peace and against the instigators of war'. A united front embracing also 'mass national liberation, religious-democratic and pacifist organisations and their adherents'.[10]

Pollitt put the new line over to the upper echelons of the CPGB in a speech to the London District Committee in October, an abbreviated report of which appeared in the *Labour Monthly* of that date. He, too, found it necessary to insist that there was no essential difference between the old and the new line. The latter was no more than 'an extension' of the old. In the next breath he contradicted himself, saying that it was an 'entirely new tactic'. It was a new tactic resulting, not from weakness, not from the defeats suffered by the working class and the communist movement, but, on the contrary, from the vast difference between 1920 and 1935 : a difference which, according to Pollitt, lay in the existence of 'firmly united communist parties in 40 capitalist countries'. The fact that the largest of these parties, next to the Russian, had been virtually wiped out, did not come into the picture; because Pollitt's central point was that the change (which was not a change, only an 'extension') was made from strength and not from weakness. Hence,

The new tactical line of the Seventh Congress of the Communist International has not been determined by any opportunist reasons. It has been determined by the consciousness that the formation and strengthening of the united front is now the main link in the chain towards the successful carrying through of the world revolution.

There is here no questioning of the past, no admission of error, no discussion – simply an about-turn to an ultra-right policy 'determined by the consciousness' that all and sundry must now be united in the forward march to world revolution. But what, then, had determined this consciousness? Pollitt supplies the answer :

Therefore, we of the Communist Party of Great Britain, in line with every section of the Communist International, *support 100 per cent, and without any reservations, everything that the Soviet Union does in its foreign policy*, because we understand that this foreign policy is in accord with the interests of the international interests of the working class as a whole and is helping forward to the path of revolution [emphasis added].

The party promptly executed the right-about-turn. The slogan 'For Soviet Britain' gave way to the slogan 'For a Labour Government'. Without a blush, Pollitt now trotted out the argument that he and his colleagues, on the insistence of Moscow, had so often denounced as counter-revolutionary Trotskyism:

> The overwhelming majority of the masses of this country who are organised in the co-operatives, the Labour Party and the trade unions are still under the influence of the Labour Party. It is not Maxton they see, it is not Baldwin they see, it is not Pollitt they see, it is the Labour Party they see, and the possibilities of a Labour Government, and the sooner we recognise it the better.

In the 1935 general election (14 November) the party put up only two candidates, both in mining constituencies. Elsewhere it campaigned for the Labour candidates. The party's two candidates were Gallacher, who won the western division of Fifeshire by 13,462 votes against the Labour candidate Adamson's 12,869 (the Tory polled 9,667); and Pollitt, in Rhondda (East), who polled 13,655 against Labour's 22,088 in a straight contest (Horner had been the party's candidate there on the three previous occasions).

In accord with the new line, the party now again applied for affiliation to the Labour Party, promising that if accepted it would abide loyally by majority decisions, with the proviso that such decisions must be in the interests of the working class. The Labour Party national executive rejected the application and the matter was debated at the Edinburgh conference in 1936. The mover of the resolution for affiliation, a delegate from the Edinburgh Trades and Labour Council, disclaimed 'any intimate association' with the CPGB, but in the course of his speech wondered if it was 'only an accident that the National Council should speak with the voice of Goebbels?'[11] This gibe, typical of the style adopted during the 'third period', shows that it was not easy for some communists (or their supporters) to switch over and use language appropriate to the new line.

Support for the resolution came from Will Lawther of the Miners' Federation. The communists had helped them, he said, in their campaign for higher wages; they had distributed union literature, going to seaside places and resorts that the union itself could not reach. Moreover, communist delegates at his union's annual conference had pledged themselves, if affiliation was granted, to abide by the Labour Party constitution. The Miners' Federation had therefore decided to support affiliation.

The voting was 592,000 for affiliation and 1,728,000 against. The result was some advance on Aneurin Bevan's motion in 1934 (referring back the executive's report on 'listed', i.e. banned, organisations) which had received only 89,000 votes; but this was a product of internal politics of the mining unions much more than an indication of support for the new party line.

The general effects of the economic crisis, the shock of the destruction of the German working-class movement, and the outbreak of the Spanish civil war, induced a leftward mood both of organised labour and among intellectuals. There arose a wider and deeper questioning of the theory and practice of reformism, of gradual yet steady and permanent advance towards the promised land through trade unionism, co-operation, and parliamentary measures to ensure a 'more equal' distribution of wealth. Had not the nazi victory shown that the employing class would not keep to the rules of the democratic game if by so doing it lost its power to exploit the workers? Franco's military assault on the Spanish 'popular front' government in the summer of 1936 enlarged the number of those who answered this question affirmatively. The expansion of this assault into full-scale civil war and the intervention of Germany and Italy on Franco's side, rallied behind the Spanish government a broad body of support – including liberals of all classes and all parties. At the same time the evident sympathy for Franco of most conservative upholders of capitalism served to create an atmosphere favourable to a non-class view of the social conflict. The communist policy of the 'people's front,' eventually known as the popular front, blossomed in this atmosphere, which it helped to create and which it enhanced. The class struggle was suspended; now the forces in conflict were, on the one side, the fascists and warmongers, and on the other the antifascists and peace-lovers, classified under the category of 'all men of goodwill'. The occasional incantation of revolutionary catchwords, and assurance that the revolutionary aim had not been lost sight of, sufficed to keep the party faithful in line.

With this left-reformist stance the prospects for the party looked brighter. Membership began to pick up, but the campaign for 'a single mass political party of the working class' was obviously getting nowhere. As long as the party remained numerically weak, its appeals for unity with the mighty battalions of the Labour Party cut no ice. At the beginning of 1936 Pollitt explained to the CC that there could be no question of just building up the Labour Party. This was not, he said, a question of time, but of principle. There was far too much 'complacency towards the all too slow growth of the Communist Party'. 'We must time and time again prove in deeds that the cause of unity is the cause of the *Communist Party*, and that this is best advanced, the more powerful the Communist Party becomes.' But would this not weaken the Labour Party? Not at all, Pollitt answered : 'the strengthening of the Communist Party is the best way to strengthen the Labour Party and the whole movement.'[12]

Having now a free hand to approach any group of people displaying the requisite goodwill in the cause of unity, the party now got together with Stafford Cripps's Socialist League and the ILP. The Socialist League had been set up mainly by ex-ILPers who had opposed their party's disaffiliation from the Labour Party in 1932. Cripps had something of a reputation as a left-winger, an opponent of gradualism and also of 'violent' revolution, advocating the revolutionary overthrow of capitalism by constitutional means. Notwithstanding this extremism, he was a figure of considerable standing in the labour movement. It was therefore regarded by the party as a step forward when he was roped into the unity campaign through the formation of a Unity Committee consisting of representatives of the CPGB (Dutt and Pollitt), the ILP (Maxton and Brockway), and the Socialist League (Cripps and Mellor).

The communists played the dominant role in this short-lived marriage, more exactly a *ménage à trois*. The manifesto issued by this committee, entitled *The Unity Campaign* (of which Maxton wrote 5 pages, Cripps 7, and Pollitt 14) contained the following key paragraph :

To save the people of the world from the growing menace of fascist aggression, the working class must mobilise the maximum effective opposition; it must mobilise for the maintenance of peace, for the defence of the Soviet Union and its fight for peace, and for a pact between Great Britain, the Soviet Union, France and all other states in which the working class have political freedom.

This paragraph summed up the basic aim of all communist propaganda and activity at the time. Everything was subordinate and geared to the aim of a pact between the 'freedom-loving, non-aggressive' states and the Soviet Union. Fenner Brockway, in his book *Inside the Left*, tells how the ILP's objection to the original wording of this paragraph nearly broke up the Unity Committee before its campaign had been launched.

Cripps and Mellor proposed that the 'Peace Front' should be limited to democratic countries, and the clause was amended to read 'states in which the working class have political freedom', but this did not satisfy us – we were in favour of a pact only between *working class* governments. On the subject of Russia's 'fight for peace' we were adamant; we did not regard its foreign policy as either socialist or peace-making.[13]

For their part, the CP representatives were equally adamant; they would not sign unless this clause was retained. Cripps brought his brilliant legal mind to bear on the problem, and solved it. The ILP representatives should record their reservations on this matter in a private letter to him, Cripps. The communists were reluctant to accept this, says Brockway, but finally yielded. So the cause of unity was saved. On behalf of the ILP, Maxton, Brockway and Jowett signed the manifesto with the offending words retained. The ILPers had salved their consciences, in private; in public they had subscribed to the view that the Soviet toilers were politically free and their government 'peace-loving', a view to which they were 'adamantly' opposed.

The net result of the Unity Committee's activities was a further weakening of the moribund ILP, to the benefit of the CPGB, and the dissolution of the Socialist League, which was dis-affiliated from the Labour Party in January. In order to prevent the expulsion of its membership *en bloc*, it disbanded itself in

March. Thus vanished the only body within the Labour Party offering some possibility of revolutionary socialist propaganda against the reformist policy of that party itself and of the communist 'cells' within it. (A large section of the Socialist League had opposed the Unity Committee on revolutionary socialist grounds.)

In 1936 there was a change in the rules of the Labour Party constitution, which provided for the direct and separate election of constituency representatives on the national executive. This became operative for the October 1937 voting. D.N.Pritt,[14] Stafford Cripps and Harold Laski – all supporters of the unity campaign – were elected to the executive. Since the distance separating Pritt from the CPGB was not wider than a split hair, the fruits of the new party policy were beginning to ripen.

9.
The People's Front

On 7 and 8 December 1935, a Congress of Peace and Friendship with the USSR was held in London, and attended by 773 delegates claiming to represent more than a million and a half people. A report of this congress was published in 1936 under the title *Britain and the Soviets*. The occasion is of interest since it offers one of the best examples of the successful application of the popular front line by the CPGB.

The names of those who took a leading part in the congress make an impressive list. Lord Listowel, Robert Boothby MP, George Bernard Shaw, F.Seymour Cocks MP, Beatrice Webb, Sir John Maynard, Viscount Hastings, Mrs Cecil Chesterton, Lord Marley, Dr Edith Summerskill, Dr Maude Royden, John Jagger, Professor P.M.S.Blackett, Vyvyan Adams MP, were among those on the platform[1] with such well-known CP members as Shapurji Saklatvala, Andrew Rothstein, the Hon. Ivor Montagu, and D.F. Springhall. The Soviet ambassador, M.Maisky, also graced the proceedings with his presence.

Even more remarkable than the gathering together of such a galaxy of political, literary and scientific talents were the views expressed. In a brief address of welcome, Lord Listowel expressed his conviction that social progress would be furthered by the course of scientific study that would be afforded the delegates. The chairman, Robert Boothby, dissociated himself from Bolshevism, but said that it would be 'foolish to ignore the note of practical realism which has been struck in the Kremlin ever since Mr Stalin came to power'. He believed that, in spite of many faults and cruelties, experiments were being carried out in Russia in the social, economic, and political fields that might well prove to be of infinite value to humanity in the future. Bernard Shaw, in the course of a speech abounding in political half-truths and amusing nonsense, confidently asserted that all the Russian people asked for was more communism. Seymour Cocks, speaking 'with a feeling of great responsibility', explained Mr Litvinov's viewpoint in almost Mr Litvinov's own words, pointing out that the Soviet Union had expressed its peaceful intentions by concluding pacts of non-aggression with Finland, Estonia, Latvia, Lithuania and Poland. A letter from the Bishop of London was then read; the bishop considered that notwithstanding the Soviet government's attitude towards Christianity, its contribution to the cause of peace should be welcomed. Lord Allen of Hurtwood, formerly Clifford Allen and a leading figure in the ILP, then moved a resolution declaring the congress's 'deepest appreciation of the Soviet Union's efforts to promote world peace, particularly by upholding the Covenant of the League of Nations', and calling for the closest possible co-operation between Great Britain and the USSR. This was seconded by a Mr Marshall, introduced as 'a capitalist', with a plea for more trade with Russia. In the course of the ensuing brief discussion, Saklatvala assured the delegates that the Red Army could not by its very nature be made to 'pinch' anyone else's land, even if Stalin wanted to, which it went without saying he did not. The resolution was then carried unanimously.

Mr Sidney Webb's contribution also signally failed to provide that 'course of scientific study' so rashly promised by Lord Listowel:

> All the people [in the USSR] are eager for greater production. This never happens in any other country.
>
> There is no unemployment in the USSR . . . There is no compulsion. People need not work if they do not want to, but then they won't get any wages or purchasing power; therefore people prefer to work. They have the choice of jobs, and there is no compulsion on them to take any particular place.
>
> There is no unemployment among actors in the USSR.
>
> You get a regular enthusiasm for more production among the workers. They go mad [sic!] in their desire and determination to turn out more stuff . . . to work harder . . . They cry for piece work.

Following this, Sir John Maynard dealt in an almost equally enthusiastic manner with the subject of collective farms; but to his own question Why did people accept the collective system? he replied by sketching the situation of the peasantry under tsarism, devoting to his subject proper so few words that they occupied less than eight lines of the printed report. There was not even a hint that the Soviet government had used a certain amount of compulsion in collectivising agriculture;[2] but this omission was compensated for by a quotation from Lenin that had nothing to do with the matter.

After Mr Jagger, then president of the National Union of Distributive and Allied Workers, had demonstrated to the satisfaction of all present the superiority of Russian over British trade unions, Professor Blackett, speaking on science in the USSR, explained why Soviet citizens were taking to tennis and dancing – 'the ordinary ballroom dancing'. This, he said, was considered by some people 'to be inconsistent with socialism'.

> They confuse the fact that, while in the early days after the Revolution there was a very natural reaction against many bourgeois forms of existence, now with the success of the Revolution ensured, many activities which had become more or less accidentally associated with capitalism again came into play.

Having cleared up this misunderstanding and made all breathe easier to know that tennis and dancing were not incompatible with socialism, he proceeded to his main theme, science. The Russians were doing good work in many branches: 'the technique is various, some good, some bad, some better and some worse than, say, in my own laboratory.' However, on central heating they were definitely ahead of everyone else. But one of the difficulties of Soviet science was a lack of trained men: 'Science is rather more difficult to force than industrial technique.' Soviet science as a whole, though, was very much like our own; differences existed but they were not essential. This was the sum of Professor Blackett's information on this subject. He made up for its meagreness by giving some information on living standards.

> I was staying with a scientist at Kharkov, and I could judge the standard of life. They get on the average about 1,000 roubles a month. They have a three-roomed flat, enough food, a maid to do the housework, and they have enough money for a holiday in the Caucasus or the Crimea most years.

He had also visited 'two Soviet rest-houses' and had come to the conclusion that 'there were also many others, equally as fine, for factory workers, for the Red Army, in fact for everyone', although he confessed he had not actually seen all these with his own eyes. He could not say the exact number of workers staying in these rest-houses and therefore confined himself to the statement that 'a million workers spend their holidays in this fashion'.

Dr Maude Royden followed the professor, apologising for 'butting in like this', but being called upon to speak was as much a surprise to her as to the audience. As she had had this sprung on her, she had not had time to consult other religious representatives whom she believed were present, but none of these dissented when she said : 'We Christians see realised in actual fact in Russia, several of the most important teachings of our Master, in whose realisation in this country we have almost ceased to believe.'

Dr Edith Summerskill, speaking on health in the USSR, was able to assert without reservation, as a result of a six-weeks' tour there, that the Soviet health services were in every respect first class, and those in capitalist Britain primitive by comparison. She was amazed by what she had seen in the hospitals there.

> The operating theatres were perfect. They do some rather extraordinary things. In some of the operating theatres, there were four people being operated on at the same time, and as they generally use a local anaesthetic, it is rather amazing to think of other patients who are having their tummy [sic] opened being able to watch another patient have a leg chopped off.

Other speakers delivered addresses of a like kind on Soviet sport, Soviet art and Soviet literature. There followed a short 'discussion', during which D.F.Springhall,[3] representing the London District of the CPGB, took part. He referred to the 'very moving tribute to the Soviet Union from one of the leading exponents of Christianity [Dr Maude Royden], whose sincerity no one could question', and declared that 'the championship of the Soviet Union was not the preserve of the communists alone; it is the prerogative of the whole of the progressive forces of humanity.'

This congress has been dealt with at some length, as it brings out very clearly the kind of activity that now occupied party organisers and propagandists; the motley collection of people they gathered together, people of eminence in their particular sphere of life, who had achieved social status, all welcome no matter what their politics so long as they were ready to express 'friendship' for the Soviet Union and to 'defend' it, however inanely. At this congress there were, according to the report, 231 trade unionists, 25 representatives of religious bodies, 60 from 'peace societies', 18 from professional bodies, 37 from local Labour Parties – all there to listen to the eminent worthies on the platform sponsored by the communists; to listen and applaud and then go back to their organisations and report that all was going wonderfully well in the fight for peace. The effect of such exercises was to demoralise the workers.

Among the leaders of the CPGB no one welcomed the new line more heartily than Gallacher MP, returned in the general election of 1935. Writing in the *Labour Monthly* of February 1936, he set at rest suspicions that he might side with the Maxton group and 'thereby become an added source of irritation' to the Labour Party. He had no intention of associating with such people. The Seventh CI Congress had given him clear guidance for his work in the House of Commons and he had applied for the Labour Party whip in the interest of unity of all forces against the National government. Although he had not actually been accorded the whip, it had not, he wrote, been refused him in any real meaning of the word. He understood the situation and much appreciated the decision of the executive of the parliamentary Labour Party that Mr Attlee should have a chat with him and explain matters. Mr Attlee struck him, Gallacher, as a 'clean, straight and likeable colleague', and he 'should make a capable leader if there is efficient team-work developed in the Labour Party'. Gallacher the one-time revolutionary then chided Sir Stafford Cripps for adopting an attitude that was 'directed towards weakening support for the League of Nations and collective security'; urged Maxton to take up a 'better attitude towards the Labour Party'; and shook an admonitory finger at that party for its tolerance of 'all kinds of individuals views'. A sad decline for that once fiery rebel, disciple of the marxist propagandist, John Maclean.

The Fourteenth Congress of the CPGB, which took place from 29 to 31 May 1937, was thus able to record considerable progress. The unity campaign was now supported by the South Wales Miners' Federation, the National Union of Distributive and Allied Workers, and the executive committee of the Amalgamated Society of Locomotive Engineers and Firemen, as well as a very large number of trade-union branches and other local sections of national organisations. Membership of the party had doubled since the previous congress and now stood at 12,500 (12,250 elsewhere in the report). Over one million copies of various pamphlets had been issued in the course of the year, and the weekly print of the *Daily Worker* had risen from 180,000 to 425,000. It was claimed that party literature sales had been 'unprecedented in the history of the labour movement', and that the party's 'mass influence had so greatly increased that our most bitter opponents are compelled to recognise the Communist Party as a political factor to be reckoned with'.[4]

The overthrow of the capitalist social system was no longer on the agenda. Fascism was not an expression of the decay of that order, of the failure of bourgeois democracy to ensure the power of the ruling class; rule by naked force, the destruction of all working-class organisation, was not inherent in the system itself, an ever present peril so long as that system existed. War likewise was not an inevitable consequence of the world struggle for markets, control of raw materials and investment areas, not to be done away with short of the social revolution. War resulted from the aggressive nature of certain states. All that was therefore needed was firm support for the League of Nations, unity of the 'non-aggressive' nations, unity of all and sundry who declared themselves 'against' fascism, 'against' war.

The extent to which the party went to 'hush up the class struggle' can be seen from the following extract from the report of the Fourteenth Congress:

> Teachers, doctors, and other professional workers, small shopkeepers and traders, small farmers and market gardeners, civil servants and local government officials, scientific workers and intellectuals generally can be brought to realise that their own interests are harmed by the interests of the millionaires and the millionaires' National government. They see that under fascism, science, education and culture generally are being destroyed and they have everything to lose by the outbreak of war.
>
> That a new political awakening has begun amongst these sections of the population is clear . . . it has received its finest expression in the support of many radicals and liberals for the Spaniards struggling for democracy and peace. Such a political awakening, with its tendencies towards a people's front . . . is a sign to be welcomed by the working class. Every encouragement should be given especially to the radical sections of the middle-class, professionals and intellectuals, to take an active part in the various forms of the peace movement, in the defence of civil liberties.[5]

Increasing emphasis was now placed on the need for a people's front. Powerful support for this came from G.D.H.Cole, one of the Labour Party's foremost intellectuals, an extremely influential author of many books on labour politics and history. He did not engage in the CP–ILP–SL unity campaign; as he explained, not because he did not agree with its purpose, but because he did not desire to court expulsion from the Labour Party. In his 1937 Left Book Club publication, *The People's Front*, he put his attitude towards the CP thus:

> Bevin and Dalton, as well as Citrine and Middleton, appear to have gone quite mad. For it is sheer madness, with the world as it is, to go tilting at communist windmills, instead of girding up their loins for a fight against the forces of reaction. It is impossible to be against capitalism, and against the communists too, as a matter of immediate policy. It is possible to be against communism, and regard the communists as erring brothers. But it is impossible to regard them as enemies – unless capitalists and even fascists are thereby to be regarded as friends. There *are* only two sides in war; and the whole world is on the brink of war.

Since those hardheaded politicos had in Cole's opinion all gone mad, there was not much point in telling them what they could and what they could not be 'against'. But Cole had understandably lost patience with these people; understandably, because for him the issue was so simple : the communists are against fascism, the immediate danger, therefore they are your allies, since you also are against fascism. There are only two sides in war – our side and their side.

On the face of it, this argument appears to be cast-iron. There is, however, another and fundamentally different way of looking at the matter; one perhaps more difficult to appreciate, but one which has been justified by what actually happened. The revolutionary socialist holds that it is not enough to be 'against' fascism; the essential question is, What are you *for*? Fascism itself is not a self-contained entity, something, as it were, materialised out of thin air : it is a political expression of capitalism in decay. The destruction of fascism, or nazism, can be accomplished, and still leave standing the social order that caused it; still leave everpresent the threat of its recurrence. The permanent crisis of world capitalism impels it to seek a political solution in the resort to rule by naked force in one form or another. Entangled in its own contradictions, the system becomes less and less able to satisfy social necessities, social demands. Each acute phase of the permanent crisis poses ever more sharply the problem of maintaining power in face of pressures from working people seeking their own way out through collective action that indirectly challenges the social order itself. A revolutionary consciousness begins to spread; revolutionary groups arise that are not abstractly 'anti-capitalist' but concretely *for* the reconstruction of society as a co-operative, classless commonweal.

A fresh impetus to the communist people's front illusion was given with the establishment, by the Gollancz publishing concern in May 1936, of the Left Book Club, which published a large number of books by leaders of the CPGB and its close sympathisers. Among these books were Dutt's *World Politics*; *Soviet Democracy* by Pat Sloan; *The Post-War History of the British Working*

Class by Allen Hutt; Wal Hannington's *The Distressed Areas*; Emile Burns' *A Handbook of Marxism; Soviet Policy and its Critics* by J.R.Campbell; *Spain in Revolt* by Gannes and Reppard; *A Philosophy for a Modern Man* by Professor H.Levy; and a special, cheap edition of the Webbs' *Soviet Communism*. These books were published as selected 'books of the month' at the low price to club members of 2s 6d (12½p). They were chosen by a panel consisting of Laski, Strachey and Gollancz. The aim of the Left Book Club was stated to be

> to help in the terribly urgent struggle *for* world peace and a better social and economic order and *against* fascism by giving to all who are determined to play their part in this struggle such *knowledge* as will immensely increase their efficiency.

In addition to the books a sizeable monthly journal, *The Left News*, was issued free to members. Groups of members were established in various parts of the country and regular meetings were held to discuss the books published.

This organisation, which by the summer of 1937 boasted 46,000 members, proved an excellent channel for the dissemination of CP views. In effect it became, between 1936 and 1939, an auxiliary of the CPGB for propaganda and recruitment purposes. Of the three members of the book selection panel, Gollancz was the least politically engaged. The unspeakable barbarities of nazism profoundly affected him emotionally, and he saw in the communists their most resolute and uncompromising enemies. The other two members of the panel were outstanding intellectual figures in the labour movement; it could not be said of them that they were politically naive, as Gollancz was. Strachey, a man with a wide knowledge of socialist theory and history and a brilliant populariser of marxist ideas, wrote regularly for the *Daily Worker* from 1935 to 1939, and could be regarded as effectively a party member. Laski's position was less clear cut and reflected more expediency than agreement. If nothing else, it showed the influence among intellectuals of the party's ultra-right line.

Reviewing the Edinburgh conference of the Labour Party in the *Labour Monthly* of November 1936, Laski argued strongly for the right of the Communist Party to affiliate to that organisation:

> the proof of Communist sincerity depends on an attempt to work with them ... I think that the Communist Party's affiliation to the Third International is a definite stumbling block unless the party agrees that, after admission to the Labour Party, it will accept the latter's decisions in preference to any made at Moscow.

At a conference organised by the party (ostensibly as a discussion meeting of *Labour Monthly* readers) in March 1937, two months after the opening of the second Moscow Trial, Laski continued to press the claims of the party to be accepted as a genuine expression of a section of the British labour movement.

> My presence on this platform with Mr Dutt symbolises, I think, the possibility of real unity within the Labour Movement ... If there is anyone by whom my writings have been more bitterly criticised in the last ten or twelve years I do not know him.

After saying that the national executive of the Labour Party was 'angry with the communists because of our internecine struggles of the past twenty years', he continued:

> I cannot share either their fears or their anger. I think that the communists have made mistakes in the past. I think, even, they are swallowing some of their errors with an amusing, even an attractive ingenuity. But whether they be seven thousand, or ten thousand, I recognise that division from them is a source of weakness, that in the policy today of Pollitt, of Dutt, of Dimitrov, there is a large measure of common ground that it is our business jointly to occupy. I think that unity means strength. I think it could give the lead we require.

Symptomatic of the party's increasing attraction for the British intellectuals was the publication in the *Daily Worker* of February 1937 of an article by Stephen Spender entitled 'I Join the Communist Party'. Born to the liberal tradition, a poet profoundly sensitive to man's inhumanity to man, heart-stricken by the countless tragedies of the depression years and outraged by the bestialities of nazism and fascism, and, as he put it, 'the lack of horror in the face of horror', Spender had already, in his book *Forward From Liberalism*, voiced his sense of loss and bewilderment, his search for something solid to hold on to in a quaking world. This book, published by the Left Book Club in 1937, contained some mild doubts about the justice of the Moscow Trials, and on this and other grounds, was criticised by J.R.Campbell in the *Daily Worker*.[6]

Replying to this criticism in his *Daily Worker* article, Spender wrote that

> Some time before the book appeared I had read the rest of the evidence, i.e. the Soviet reports of the Moscow trials, and I became convinced that there undoubtedly had been a gigantic plot against the Soviet government and that the evidence was true. However, it was too late for me to alter my book.

This statement was obviously made less as a result of conviction arising from a serious investigation of the matter (which was perhaps beyond his capacity and inclination), than from the insistence of Pollitt. Spender would not have been admitted to membership of the party unless he had made this statement. Having made it and joined the party, he had rendered the Stalinists the best service of which he was capable; no effort was thereafter made to integrate him into the daily activity of a member; he was required only as another bit of decoration for the party's popular front facade. In due course Spender, too, realised that he had been duped.

As international tension mounted with each stride forward of nazi aggression so the Stalinists set their sails to catch every breath of wind favourable to their new course. Class-war agitation was shelved and all possible allies were welcomed to the 'anti-fascist' front, regardless of political conviction, so long as they did not question the infallibility of Stalin. Anxious to dispel any lingering doubts about the sincerity of the party's conversion to liberalism, a resolution of the CC in September 1937 explained that 'the dictatorship of the proletariat', although remaining party doctrine, since after all it meant no more than 'a very broad form of democracy for the working people', was not to be referred to in future : 'we need to make it clear that this issue is not now on the order of the day in the present situation in Britain.'[7] A further noteworthy expression of the party's accommodation to bourgeois politics was the argument used by the CC in a statement of 19

March 1938 (*Save London from the Fate of Barcelona*) that the Chamberlain government was 'working towards a fascist Spain, and thereby threatening the communications vital to British interests . . .'[8] This echoed the view taken by some conservatives, and broadly hinted at by Churchill, for whom it was of course perfectly legitimate to fight against fascism, on the ground that it was a threat to Britain's imperial interests.

In a like manner the party now posed as the stalwart champion of religious bodies persecuted by the fascists. Pollitt wrote in the *Labour Monthly* of October 1938 that

> Among protestants and catholics there is uneasiness at the brutal and repressive methods that fascism adopts to prevent religious teaching and expression, and resentment that Chamberlain's policy helps the fascists to carry through their attack upon religion by force.

Having spent some years vociferously insisting that it made no difference to the workers whether they suffered under bourgeois democracy or under fascism, Pollitt now wrote : 'There have even been some in the communist ranks who have talked as though we were indifferent to the form of capitalist rule.' Such erring members, and others, should 'take the trouble to find out what the workers suffer in fascist countries'.

In March 1938 the people's front gained another powerful recruit. On the twentieth of that month the editor of *Reynold's News*, Sidney Elliott, published an appeal for a United Peace Alliance under the leadership of the Labour Party for the defeat of Chamberlain. The proposal was that all the opposition forces, labour, liberal, co-operative, ILP, independent, and communist, should combine in a supreme effort to bring down the government. At the Easter Conference of the Co-operative Party a resolution was passed, by 2,343,000 votes to 1,947,000, declaring that

> in view of the grave international situation, the dangers of a world war, fascist dictatorship, aggression encouraged by the foreign policy of the present government, it is essential to replace the government at the earliest opportunity if peace is to be secured and the rights of democracy in Britain safeguarded.

The Stalinists, who had been most active behind the scenes in promoting the resolution, hailed it as a signal victory. In a speech to the London District Committee on 11 June, Pollitt said that it had not been possible at the party congress in May to deal with the question of the People's Front other than in general terms, but that now 'The People's Front, the United Peace Alliance, call it what you will, has become the main issue in British politics.' He denied that this was 'some newly devised tactic thrust upon us because of the advent of fascism'; on the contrary, 'The basic principle of the People's Front is the same basic principle underlying the whole theory and practice of Leninism, the need for seeking allies to carry forward the struggle as a whole.'[9]

Communist Party support for this Peace Alliance went so far to the right that it even attacked the Labour Party executive for not agreeing to support the Liberal Party in a by-election at Aylesbury in May 1938. For years the Stalinists had been constantly smelling out plots for Liberal – Labour alliances and denouncing them as treachery to socialism. Now the Stalinists themselves were denouncing the Labour Party for *not* coming to an arrangement with the Liberal Party. Not stopping at denunciation, they took their supporters out of the Aylesbury Labour Party and formed a so-called Progressive Peace Alliance, whose task was to campaign for the Liberal candidate. Pollitt, who not long since had pledged his party to abide by the constitution and discipline of the Labour Party if it was permitted to affiliate, appealed to all men of goodwill to vote Liberal. Reactionary forces were at work to divide the lovers of peace and the defenders of liberty, Pollitt declared. These 'reactionary forces' were vaguely defined as 'a certain group at Transport House', backed up by the 'Cliveden Set'.[10] The CPGB issued thousands of leaflets denigrating the Labour candidate and urging the electorate to vote Liberal to demonstrate the people's will towards a Peace Alliance. Yet in the event the Labour candidate (whom the liberal *Manchester Guardian* considered had jeopardised his chances by 'preaching the entire socialist doctrine') raised the Labour vote by 3,000, while the Tory vote dropped by 3,033 and the Liberal by 2,871, in what the *Daily Worker* itself admitted was a heavy poll.[11] However, this result did not give the Communist Party pause. The result would not, the *Daily Worker* commented, save Transport House 'from conviction as enemies of peace and security for presenting a seat to Chamberlain. . . .'

How was it that the rank and file of the CPGB did not see the gulf between communist principles and the party's political line? Of course the membership fluctuated; the disheartened and the disillusioned dropped out, among them some who did recognise the gulf between principle and practice. The losses were more than made good by the influx of 'popular-fronters' attracted precisely by the policy of liberalism. But what of the hard core who regarded the party as still pursuing its revolutionary purpose? How did they persuade themselves?

The answer to this appears most clearly in the varying attitudes adopted by the party on the issue of the Second World War to which we now turn.

10.
Left-Right, Right-Left

The Sixth Congress of the Comintern (July – August 1928) had laid down in considerable detail the communist attitude towards war. The theses adopted on this question were published in 1932 by the CPGB under the heading, 'The Struggle against Imperialist War and the Tasks of the Communists' in a pamphlet entitled *The Attitude of the Proletariat to War.*

The argument proceeded from the standpoint that war was the inevitable outcome of capitalist exploitation, necessarily involving incessant rivalry for market outlets, control of sources of raw materials, and spheres of investment. War could therefore not be abolished short of the abolition of the regime that produced it; any other anti-war theories and activities served only to foster illusions and seriously weaken the real struggle. A vigorous fight must be waged against the various shades of pacifism; 'official pacifism', expressed in the League of Nations, Locarno, disarmament conferences, etc; socialist pacifism, which is the same as official pacifism, but embellished with socialist and even marxist phrases; left-socialist pacifism, which indulges in meaningless phrases and often lays 'excessive stress upon the destructiveness of modern weapons; semi-religious pacifism, 'which has its basis in the church movement'; and co-operative pacifism, exemplified chiefly in the International Co-operative Alliance.[1] While all these 'pacifist swindlers must be relentlessly exposed and combated', the anti-war sentiments of the masses must be taken into consideration, the workers must be made to understand the falseness of such slogans 'No More War', 'General Strike against the declaration of war', etc. 'The proletariat, however, supports and conducts national revolutionary wars and socialist wars against imperialism . . .'[2]

It was also made clear that

> The peace policy of the proletarian state does not imply that the Soviet state has become reconciled with capitalism . . . The proletariat in the Soviet Union harbours no illusions as to the possibility of a durable peace with the imperialists. The proletariat knows that the imperialists' attack against the Soviet Union is inevitable; that in the process of a proletarian world revolution wars between proletarian and bourgeois states, wars for the emancipation of the world from capitalism, will *necessarily* and *inevitably* arise.[3]

In the same year the party published these statements of uncompromising opposition to all sorts of pacifism, in which it proclaimed the necessity and inevitability of war between proletarian and bourgeois states, it was engaged in organising a world anti-war congress supported by a host of pacifists of all varieties.[4] The occasion was the Russian response to the Japanese invasion of Manchuria (18-19 September 1931) which was seen by Moscow as part of the world imperialists' interventionist plot against the Soviet Union.

During the period immediately preceding the change-over to the People's Front policy the party had a difficult job trying to work out exactly what the Soviet government was up to, and, consequently, how it should respond. This is exemplified in an article in the *Labour Monthly* of November 1934 by R.F.Andrews (A.Rothstein), where he wrote:

> If Socialists ought to support the Soviet Union's work in the League [of Nations], for that very reason it follows that they should oppose the Labour Party's conception of the League as a 'collective peace system'.
>
> Nor is it true that, as Henderson stated, the Soviet government considers the League 'a force for peace'. Stalin a year ago said it may be 'somewhat of an obstruction that could, even to a certain extent, hinder the outbreak of war'.

Consequently, Andrews concluded, 'Every worker who values peace must join, without delay and with *all his energies, in exposing and fighting the Labour Party's war policy tooth and nail*'. But four months later there was the communiqué issued on the conclusion of Eden's visit to Moscow (March 1935), which ran, in part:

> Mr Eden and MM Stalin, Molotov, and Litvinov were of the opinion that in the present international situation it was more than ever necessary to pursue the endeavour to promote the building of a system of collective security in Europe . . . in conformity with the principles of the League of Nations.[5]

The representatives of the two governments 'were happy to note, as a result of a full and frank exchange of views, that there is at present no conflict of interests between the two governments on any of the main issues of international policy.'[6]

A change of policy was evidently in the offing. The change received the official seal of approval at the Seventh Congress of the Comintern (August 1935) and so, when war broke out, the CPGB quite naturally assumed that the new policy required that they should support it.

On 2 September 1939, the *Daily Worker* published the party's manifesto on the war. This set forth, under 14 headings, a series of programmatic demands considered vital for the successful prosecution of the war (one of which echoed the Bolshevik demand for a peace without annexations or indemnities). The party here declared its 'readiness to take part in any struggle, political or military, to secure the defeat of fascism'.

This manifesto was re-published in a pamphlet by Pollitt – *How to Win the War*, issued on 14 September and called 'this masterly pamphlet' by Randall Swingler in the *Daily Worker* of 15 September. It stated, *inter alia*, that

> The Communist Party supports the war, believing it to be a just war which should be supported by the whole working class and all friends of democracy.
>
> It is true that the Polish government was reactionary in its attitude to the Polish labour movement, but it is with the *people* of Poland that we are primarily concerned. If Hitler is allowed to impose his domination on Poland, the people will be forced to accept conditions infinitely worse than any thing they have yet suffered. The Nazi Party and the Gestapo will outlaw every atom of working-class organisation; tens of thousands will be murdered

or sent to concentration camps; hundreds of thousands will be exiled to forced labour in Germany; crush-taxation will be imposed to strengthen the German war machine and its next act of aggression.

In the House of Commons, Gallacher also made his personal attitude clear: 'I will stick at no sacrifice to ensure the defeat of nazi aggression';[7] and the party newspaper declared: 'You will find us helping to win the war'. On 18 September the *Daily Worker* commented on the Soviet attack against Poland with the front-page headline 'Soviet Counterblow Against the Nazis'. On 20 September its front-page headline ran 'Hitler Offers "Peace" to Split France and Britain'.

No doubt about it, the party knew precisely where it stood. Then on 28 September came the bolt from the blue – the publication of the joint Nazi-Soviet 'Declaration' on the war, in which the two states undertook to be neutral towards each other, if one of them should be involved in war. Any disputes were to be settled 'through friendly exchange of opinion'. The party discovered to its horror that all it had been saying was completely out of step with Soviet policy. It had failed to appreciate the true aim of the Nazi-Soviet pact of 23 August.

This pact had been hailed in a central committee statement as 'a victory for peace and socialism against the war plans of fascism and the pro-fascist policy of Chamberlain'.[8] No, not a crazy dream – there it was, in black and white. At the same time, it followed from this 'victory for peace and socialism' that the conclusion of 'the Anglo-Soviet pact' had become all the more urgent. And for some weird reason it was felt necessary to quote from Stalin's report to the Eighteenth Congress of the Russian party on 10 March, these words: 'Far be it from me to moralise on the policy of non-intervention, to talk of treason, treachery, and so on.' Far be it from him! The irony escaped them; they were still half-dazed from the staggering blow dealt them; all they could think about was how to put on a bold face. Soviet policy had not changed; there had been only 'a change in nazi policy'. Of course, that was it! So they carried on – till the next staggering blow – the

Nazi-Soviet declaration on the war – knocked them sideways again.

It took a little more than a month for the party to get its breath back. On 7 October a new manifesto was published in the *Daily Worker*: 'This war is not a war for democracy against fascism. It is not a war for the defence of peace against aggression.' The immediate calling of a peace conference was now demanded. Pollitt's pamphlet, *How to Win the War*, was withdrawn from circulation and he was required to take the role of scapegoat and resign the secretaryship of the party (11 October). Campbell had likewise temporarily to take a back seat. Thus a spurious air of plausibility was given to the excuse that the original manifesto had been a 'personal' one. The *Daily Worker* of 12 October announced that 'The manifesto of October 7 *corrects* the declaration of September 2' [my emphasis added]. And on 23 November Pollitt and Campbell returned from their meditations in the wilderness and publicly confessed that they had sinned in 'resisting (sic!) the line of the Communist Party and the Communist International'.

Pollitt's pamphlet having been withdrawn, it was necessary to replace it. The task was performed by Dutt, who produced *Why This War*[9] in November, from which we quote the following:

> After German fascism has been compelled by the strength of the Soviet Union to retreat from its anti-Soviet aims, the main world conflict is more and more clearly revealed between British imperialism, as the principal and most aggressive force of world reaction, and world socialism, led by the Soviet Union.
>
> Since the end of September the Soviet Union has proposed peace for western Europe. If peace is refused, it is plain to all in the present conditions that the responsibility for continuing the war will lie with the British and French ruling classes – in fact, since France is not a free agent, with the British ruling class.

The source of this argument is not far to seek. The *Joint Declaration of the Soviet and German Governments* contains the following words:

> The German government and the government of the USSR, having finally settled by the treaty signed today the questions arising from the dissolution of the Polish State, and having thereby created

a firm foundation for a lasting peace in eastern Europe, in mutual agreement express the opinion that the liquidation of the present war between Germany on the one hand and England and France on the other would be in the interests of all nations. Therefore both governments will direct their common efforts, if necessary in accord with other friendly powers, to attain this aim as soon as possible. If, however, these efforts of both Governments remain unsuccessful, it will be established thereby that England and France bear the responsibility for the continuation of the war, and in the event of the continuation of the war the Governments of Germany and the USSR will consult with each other on the necessary measures.[10]

Molotov's speech to the Fifth (Extraordinary) Session of the supreme Soviet on 31 October also provided Dutt with a useful key to the Soviet government's approach:

In connection with these important changes in the international situation certain old formulas, which we employed but recently, and to which many people are so accustomed, are now obviously out of date and inapplicable. We must be quite clear on this point so as to avoid making gross errors in judging the new political situation that has developed in Europe. We know, for example, that in the past few months such concepts as 'aggression' and 'aggressor' have acquired new concrete connotation, new meaning. It is not hard to understand that we can no longer employ these concepts in the sense we did, say, three or four months ago. Today, as far as the European great powers are concerned, Germany's position is that of a state which is striving for the earliest termination of war and for peace, while Britain and France, which but yesterday were declaiming against aggression, are in favour of continuing the war and are opposed to the conclusion of peace. The roles you see are changing.[11]

In drawing up the manifesto of 7 October, the party had used the Leninist formula, 'The responsibility for the present war lies *equally* on all the warring powers.' Now this was put back in the files and the responsibility laid squarely upon Britain and France, because nazi Germany was in alliance with the USSR. At the same time this alliance turned aggressors into non-aggressors and vice versa. Everything depended on how the Soviet government viewed matters. Thus communists, so-called, stood on the same ground as capitalists: both viewed war as the result of conflict between certain aggressively disposed countries against others non-aggressively disposed. So the responsibility for war lay with the aggressors and not with the capitalist system itself, that is, not equally on all the warring states. This is what the Stalinists were now teaching the workers.

Here it is worth quoting some words from Leon Trotsky, spoken shortly before the outbreak of the war:

> I do not feel it is my mission to give counsel to imperialist governments, even if they name themselves democratic, nor to the Bonapartist clique of the Kremlin, even if it names itself socialist. I can only give counsel to the workers. My counsel to them is not to believe a single instant that the war of the two imperialist camps can bring anything but oppression and reaction in both camps. It will be a war of the slave-owners who cover themselves with various masks: 'democracy', 'civilisation', on the one hand, 'race', 'honor', on the other. Only the overthrow of all slave-owners can once for all end war and open an epoch of true civilisation.[12]

From then on, until Germany invaded Russia, the party parrotted the arguments used by Molotov and other mouthpieces of Stalin. But it did not confine itself to words only. In the *Labour Monthly* of November Arthur Horner indicated the tactic to be pursued on the industrial front. The 'movement for what is an absolutely necessary defence of living standards must be co-ordinated and directed with the aim of securing a general advance', he wrote. The simple-minded viewed this as a return to the principle of the class struggle, or a genuine concern for the workers. In fact, it was no more than part of the party's campaign for peace; as soon as peace was no longer on the agenda the tactic would be dropped like a hot potato. In the meantime, peace was what the Soviet government wanted. So in the same issue of the *Labour Monthly* Dutt dutifully wrote that

> The gathering movement against war is finding its first expression in the demand for peace, for an immediate ending of the war and the calling of a peace conference. The call of the Soviet Union for peace has enormously stimulated this.

And the following month he wrote:

> the successive peace proposals have been rejected by British and French imperialism, whose aggressive aims to reduce German

imperialism to second rank, to establish their reactionary domination in Europe and to prepare for the final assault on the Soviet Union stand out ever more clearly.

In February 1940 Pollitt, now completely 'rehabilitated', contested a by-election in Silverton on an 'anti-war' platform against the Labour Party. In April once more he explained why he had changed his mind about the war:

> When the might of the Soviet Union compelled Hitler to make a pact of non-aggression with the Soviet Union, the Chamberlain government declared war on Nazi Germany, *not to crush fascism*, but to extend its own domination in Europe ... and find other means through which it could continue its anti-Soviet policy. The fundamental cause of my own mistake at the beginning of the war is that I did not see this in time, and did not realise that with the signing of the Soviet-German pact an entirely new international situation had opened up.[13]

In the February issue of the same *Labour Monthly*, however, Campbell had already said that 'the mistake' had not been merely personal, but one committed by the entire party: 'The initial mistake of the Labour Party in supporting the war was understandable, although the same cannot be said for the communist.'

Since Stalin had said, on the 29 November 1939, that it was not Germany that had attacked France and England, but the other way round; that the 'ruling circles of France and England [had] rudely rejected both Germany's peace proposals and the Soviet Unions' efforts to bring the war quickly to an end',[14] the party could not attack nazism. Instead, the party reverted to the 'third period' type of attack on the Labour Party. Hitler was holding only 90 million people in subjection, Dutt wrote, while Britain held 250 million in subjection.[15] Ivor Montagu, another of the party's intellectuals, wanted to know what the difference was between the Labour Front of Dr Ley (the nazi Minister of Labour) and the Labour Party: the British Labour leader 'does not need a rubber truncheon to make him behave in precisely the same way' as a nazi.[16] Pursuing the same analogy, R.Page Arnot wrote that in Germany there was the Labour Front, in Britain there are the trade unions. 'How many further steps have to be taken before the distinction from the Labour Front disappears?'[17] And W.Rust, writing under the heading 'National Socialism: Labour Party Brand', charged that 'the Labour leaders have become the advocates of the most extreme and ferocious measures, including the spreading of the war and provocative measures against the Soviet Union.'[18]

There was for the party obviously no question of a serious analysis of fascism as a peculiar social phenomenon, as different from Labour reformism as chalk is from cheese. They could not even admit the plain fact that the entire working-class movement in Germany had been smashed to atoms – the trade unions, the Social Democratic Party and the Communist Party – its leaders imprisoned or murdered, if not lucky enough to flee abroad. No, that would have been tantamount to questioning, if not directly attacking, Soviet policy. The Soviet government fondly believed that if a peace could be arranged the nazis would be content with what they had already seized by force of arms. The irony of this policy was that if it had succeeded Russia would have faced alone the inevitable future attack by Germany.

On 11 February 1940 a new Soviet-German trade agreement was signed, by the terms of which 'The trade turnover between Germany and the USSR in the first year . . . is to reach a figure greater than any achieved between the two countries before the world war'. Moreover, 'It is intended to increase reciprocal deliveries of goods still further in the future'.[19] These words contrast with the following from Stalin's speech at the Eighteenth Congress of the CPSU (March 1939):

> Formally speaking, the policy of non-intervention might be defined as follows: 'Let each country defend itself against the aggressors as it likes and as best it can. That is not our affair. We shall trade both with the aggressors and with their victims.' [But this attitude] means conniving at aggression, giving free rein to war and, consequently, transforming the war into a world war.[20]

The Stalinists outside Russia at first denied the existence of any such agreement to increase trade with nazi Germany, just as, some years before, they had denied that Russia supplied oil to

Italy during the war against Abyssinia; then shrugged it off as of no significance. There was another 'trade': the agreement to hand over to the Gestapo some 400 German communists who had taken refuge in Russia. When one of those so handed over (Margarete Buber-Neumann, widow of the German communist party leader and CI functionary, Heinz Neumann, who died or was murdered in a Soviet jail) disclosed this inhumanly treacherous act, the British party could not refute the evidence, so they . . . kept silent.

In August 1940 the British party laid the foundation stone of a fresh 'united front' venture by the formation of the People's Vigilance Committee, which in due course became the People's Convention. The object of this body was to broaden the anti-war appeal and create a mass movement in support of Soviet policy under the guise of a 'defence of the people's living standards', 'defence of democratic rights', 'adequate air-raid precautions', and 'a people's peace that gets rid of the causes of war' (the causes were not specified, so that the appeal should be as broad as possible).

The People's Convention was held on 12 January 1941 and attended by 2,234 delegates representing, according to the official report, 1,200,000 people in 1,304 different organisations. Pritt, introducing the policy and programme resolution, asserted that the government was 'moving steadily all along the line towards a general compulsory system of a fascist pattern', and declared that 'The fight for wages and trade-union conditions are (sic) now the very centre of the battle'. 'Our policy', he said, 'is to offer to the peoples of the enemy a peace of no annexations and no reparations or idemnities, with liberty to all peoples to determine their own destiny'. The party leaders, Dutt, Pollitt and Pat Sloan made supporting speeches. So did Krishna Menon,[21] who stated that: 'The spirit of the Indian people is with this Convention . . . There is no use asking whether you would choose British imperialism or nazism, it is like asking a fish if he wants to be fried in margarine or butter.'[22]

One cannot do better here than to quote from Trotsky's

argument in refutation of this kind of reasoning. On the question of whether there is any difference between democracy and fascism, he wrote:

> Is there a difference in the 'class content' of these two regimes? If the question is posed only as regards the *ruling class*, then there is no difference. If one takes into account the position and relation of *all* classes, from the angle of the proletariat, then the difference appears to be quite enormous.
>
> In the course of many decades, the workers have built up within the bourgeois democracy, by utilising it, by fighting against it, their own strongholds and bases of *proletarian democracy*: the trade unions, the political parties, the educational and sports clubs, the co-operatives, etc. The proletariat cannot attain power within the formal limits of bourgeois democracy, but can only do so by taking the road of revolution: this has been proved both by theory and experience. And these bulwarks of workers' democracy are absolutely essential for the taking of the revolutionary road. The work of the Second International consisted in creating just such bulwarks during the epoch when it was still fulfilling its progressive historic labour.
>
> Fascism has for its basic and only task, the razing to their foundations of all institutions of proletarian democracy. Has this any 'class meaning' for the proletariat, or hasn't it?'[23]

On 21 January the Coalition government banned publication of the *Daily Worker*, but refrained from proscribing the party itself, or from clamping down on its alternative methods of carrying on pacifist-orientated anti-war propaganda. The ban was of short duration, for on 21 June Hitler invaded the Soviet Union and on the following day the party issued a statement that among other things said:

> Hitler's attack against the socialist Soviet Union is fascism's supreme aggression against the people of the world.
>
> The cause of the Soviet Union is the cause of the working people all over the world, of freedom, of socialism.
>
> Hitler's attack will be resisted and defeated by the common action of the working people in all countries in solidarity with the Red Army, Navy and Air Force of the Soviet workers.
>
> This attack is the sequel of the secret moves which have been taking place behind the curtain of the Hess mission . . .
>
> We have no confidence in the present government dominated by

the Tory friends of fascism and Coalition Labour leaders, who have already shown their stand by their consistent anti-Soviet slander campaigns.

From the above two points emerge: a) another change in the nature of the war – another 'entirely new international situation has developed'; b) the delusion that the war was being 'switched' against the Soviet Union by the British 'Tory friends of fascism' and Labour leaders. On the first point the party was in line with Soviet policy. Stalin put them right in regard to the second when in a broadcast on 3 July he said:

> Our war for the freedom of our fatherland will merge with the struggle of the peoples of Europe and America for their independence, for democratic liberties. It will be a united front of peoples standing for freedom and against enslavement and threats of enslavement by Hitler's fascist armies.

Therefore the communists in Britain must take seriously and act upon Churchill's declaration that 'We will never parley, we will never negotiate with Hitler or any of his gang ... Any man or State who fights against Nazidom will have our aid ...' On 8 July, on behalf of the secretariat of the CPGB, Pollitt therefore circulated to all party members a statement explaining in detail the new line of the party, and demanding unconditional support of the war effort.

Two years of open struggle for a totally different policy had left its mark upon the consciousness of the rank and file. Some anxiety as to how readily they would accept yet another right-about-turn is evident in the phrasing of this document (the secrecy of which could not be preserved, since bewilderment of members led some to ask others, expelled from the party for 'trotskyism', what they thought of it). Party propaganda had been showing such complete distrust, not only of Churchill and company, but also of the entire trade-union and labour movement, that many members could be expected to be more than a little disorientated. Hence Pollitt's 'appeal to our party', a cyclostyled document of some three thousand words addressed strictly to party members only, was a compound of impassioned pleading and fervent exhortation. It began:

The dastardly attack of German fascism on the Soviet Union brought about an immediate change in the entire world situation – a change that Churchill's speech, Stalin's reply, Stalin's epoch-making speech, and Eden's declaration at Leeds, have all emphasised as representing a fundamentally new situation in which every government and every political party has had to respond with new policies and a new approach to all questions.

The Communist Party, naturally, immediately changed its political line to meet the new situation and tasks imposed upon it. It made changes that have to be carried through without mental reservations of any kind and not in any tongue-in-cheek state of mind.

It was transparently clear that 'all parties' had not had to 'respond with new policies', but the fiction was necessary in order to 'explain' why, now that Churchill and company were supporting the Soviet Union and not nazi Germany, contrary to all communist predictions, the party had to 'respond'. The 'appeal' goes on to say that 'the defeat of Hitler is *now* the supreme task' [emphasis added], and that the party now stood for a 'united national front of all those who are for Hitler's defeat'.

We are putting the issue now standing before our party so sharply because we understand the difficulties that can occur in making the adjustment (sic) of our policy to meet the new position that its urgency demands. We know that for two years our party has fought for a political line that has now to be changed; it was a policy that was correct in the circumstances, in which it was operative, but today those circumstances no longer exist.

What were the changed circumstances? The Soviet Union was under military attack and the rulers of Britain had pledged their aid to the Soviet Union.

But in our party, doubts are still being voiced that can give the impression that there is disappointment that the Churchill government has not lined up with Hitler against the Soviet Union in order to prove some theoretical point about the only line of British imperialism being to effect a switch of the war against the Soviet Union.

The next passage in the appeal reveals the full extent of the policy changes:

Undoubtedly there are forces in Britain who would like to make a switch, but they are not the dominant forces [the word 'not' was omitted from the original, obviously in error – the typist had written it that way so many times before . . .]. If, however, any sectarian attitude of the Communist Party, by standing aside and not pulling our full weight in the common effort to defeat Hitler, *any putting forward of impossible demands is permitted, any irresponsible fighting of by-elections in present conditions* [emphasis added]; then our party simply plays into the hands of the dark forces who are waiting for such an opportunity to take advantage of dissensions and splits in the national fight against fascism, opportunities that will never come if we do our job as our party can do it, when we are all in it full tilt.

This is the frankest admission ever made by the party that the policy pursued over the previous two years had not been calculated to further the cause of the working people in their class struggle. The specific warning against 'impossible' demands against 'irresponsible' fighting of by-elections, was necessary only because this was precisely what the party had been doing all along. No more of this in the future. In a by-election in Cardiff East in 1942 the party gave unqualified support to Sir James Grigg, the Tory, against the ILP candidate, Fenner Brockway. The South Wales communist organiser, Idris Cox, wrote in a letter to the *Cardiff and Suburban News* that

We communists would have liked to do more in the campaign. But while the Tories were glad to announce our support for Sir James Grigg they were reluctant to work in active co-operation with the communists. This was most unfortunate.

During the two-year period of phoney opposition to the war the Stalinists had proclaimed the 'crisis of imperialism' as the long-hoped-for opportunity for the colonial peoples in their struggle for independence. India was the very heart of this struggle. The Indian communists had been actively aided by the British party. Krishna Menon's 'margarine and butter' analogy has been noted above; superficial as it was, it more or less summed up the attitude of the party in India, which was underground, most of its leaders in jail, and altogether isolated by war conditions from the course of events. So the communists there were sticking to the view that the war had given an undreamt-of chance to strike a decisive blow against Britain, and that history would never forgive them if they did not seize it. How could they be convinced that. with the Soviet Union now under fascist attack, this attitude was incorrect? They naturally distrusted all information from official British sources and the Russians could not intervene without disclosing an influence they disclaimed. Into the breach stepped Harry Pollitt. A letter from him to the communist leaders in India was delivered through Sir Reginald Maxwell, then Home Secretary to the government of India, and this swayed the balance of the debate among them: the Indian party committed itself to support of the war.[24]

Thus the British party put into cold storage another of its 'fundamental principles'. Dutt's comparison of nazi-German imperialism with British imperialism, to the advantage of the latter, was quite forgotten and now the view was, as the party expressed it in August 1941, that

> It is felt that if the Nazis won this war then it would mean the brutal enslavement of all the colonial peoples. We must see that nothing stands in the way of all parts of the Empire co-operating with Britain and Russia in defeating the common enemy.

Government of the majority by a minority rests by its nature on force and fraud, and as the crises inherent in capitalism become ever more acute the cement of democratic fraud begins to crumble, revealing the steel core of violence that reinforces it. This violence can be ended in only one way: the conquest of political power by the majority who do the real work of the world. At the head of this movement of revolt against oppression, against a system productive only of economic and financial chaos and of social disorder, must march the organised working class, demonstrating with ever mounting force the great gulf between their actual economic power and their lack of political power.

The CPGB not only failed to propagate this socialist teaching, but taught instead the unity of the oppressed with their oppressors, the unity of 'non-aggressors' against the 'aggressors'. Moreover, the question of precisely who the 'aggressors' were depended upon the situation in which the Soviet Union found itself.

The CPGB abandoned the marxist view that war is the inevitable outcome of the rivalry for markets, spheres of investment, sources of raw materials. It therefore lined up with bourgeois democracy, with pacifists and reformists of all shades; towards the end of the war hailing 'the wisdom and statesmanship of the United Nations' leaders', which was 'yet another proof of their determination to build lasting security and prosperity for the world'.[25]

Look back on those who in 1920 and 1921 gathered together to found the Communist Party. Could they ever have conceived it possible that their party would degenerate to this – that one day its most admired and respected leader would hail 'the wisdom and statesmanship' of the ruling class?

Notes and References

1. Beginnings

1. H.Pelling, *The British Communist Party,* Black 1958; L.J.Macfarlane, *The British Communist Party: Its Origin and Development until 1929,* Macgibbon & Kee 1966; J.Klugmann, *History of the Communist Party of Great Britain,* Lawrence & Wishart, vol. 1 *1919-24,* 1968; vol. 2 *1925-26,* 1969.
2. Marx – Engels, *Selected Correspondence*, London 1934, letter 176.
3. *ibid.* p. 393, note.
4. See H.M.Hyndman, *Further Reminiscences,* 1912, pp. 259-77 for an account of the SDF's attitude.
5. The *Clarion* paper was founded in 1891 by Robert Blatchford and A.M.Thompson. The Clarion groups were loosely connected with the ILP, their main task was to promote sales of the paper and of socialist pamphlets and books. Blatchford was the author of *Britain for the British,* which had a very large sale and was responsible for converting many to socialism.
6. Attention is drawn to Nan Milton, *John Maclean,* (Pluto Press) 1973, a fine and moving account of the BSP's most outstanding figure of whom it may truly be said that he was

   'One who never turned his back but marched breast forward,
   Never doubted clouds would break,
   Never dreamed though right were worsted, wrong would triumph,
   Held we fall to rise, are baffled to fight better,
   Sleep to wake.'

7. D.DeLeon, *The Socialist Reconstruction of Society*, Socialist Labour Press, undated.
8. *ibid*, p. 23.
9. *ibid.* p. 25.
10. J.Hinton, *The First Shop Stewards' Movement,* Allen & Unwin 1973.
11. J.T.Murphy, *Preparing for Power,* first published 1934; reprinted Pluto Press 1972. (Murphy subsequently played a leading role in the CPGB, but left it in 1932.)
12. The Plebs League was formed by a number of dissidents at Ruskin College, Oxford – founded by two Americans in 1899 for working-class students. Resentful of establishment-biased teaching, the dissidents

eventually (1909) started a Labour College movement 'to equip workers to propagate and defend the interests of their class against the dominant ruling class ideas and theories . . .' Major support for this movement was given by the South Wales Miners' Federation and the NUR.

13. For Guild Socialism see M.Beer, *A History of British Socialism*, Bell & Sons 1929, vol. 2, pp. 363-72. For some material on the conflict between the 'democrats' and the 'sovietists' in the National Guild League see *The Guildsman*, no. 41, May 1920; also no. 42 (June); no. 45 (September), article by G.D.H.Cole, 'The Communist Party and the NGL', no. 42, June 1920; and Rowland Kenney, 'Our faction fight', no. 45, September 1920. Subsequent issues indicate that the debate continued and that CPGB members still maintained contact with Guild activities.

14. *Daily Herald*: launched in 1911, strongly syndicalist in tone; see Raymond Postgate, *The Life of George Lansbury*, Longmans Green 1951, – pp.134-51, for a description of its style and content in the early years of its existence.

15. It would be unnecessary to make so obvious a point were it not for the fact that there is a view still current that CPGB was somehow 'manufactured' by the Communist International. Quite apart from its failure to appreciate the continuity of the revolutionary tradition in this country, this view neglects the basic peculiarity of communist parties, as then conceived, a peculiarity distinguishing them from all other parties: the fact that they were not national parties, but sections of one world party (hence the CPGB, not the British Communist Party). This was the organisational expression of the marxist view that the new, higher, social order superseding capitalism had to be, could only be, a world order. Given this standpoint, an international 'general staff' was indispensable; its concern with the political and organisational development of the various parties, to ensure mutual assistance and common basic policy, to organise joint action and so forth – all this followed from the principle of the international character of the proletarian revolution. There was no question here of an absurd effort to conjure communist parties out of thin air. (That the attempt to maintain this International true to its original purpose failed does not render the attempt itself any the less praiseworthy and historically significant.)

16. W.Gallacher, *Communist International*, Modern Books 1927, nos. 10-12, p.1255.

17. Arthur MacManus: a fiery orator and a leading shop steward on the Clyde; died in 1927 and his ashes were interred in the Kremlin wall.

18. L.B.Kamenev: one of the Bolshevik luminaries; member of the Central Committee and the Political Bureau of the Russian party; editor of *Pravda*; first president of the Soviet Republic; with Zinoviev and Stalin made up the so-called *troika* against Trotsky after Lenin's death in

1924; broke with Stalin and joined the Left (trotskyist) Opposition in 1925; capitulated in 1927; framed up in the Kirov assassination affair (1934) (cf. H.Dewar, *Assassins at Large*, 1951, ch. 10) and shot in 1936.

19. *Official Report*, CPGB pamphlet, no date; all subsequent quotations regarding the Convention are taken from this report.

20. W.Mellor was later to become editor of the *Daily Herald*; still later of *Tribune* when it was the organ of Stafford Cripps's Socialist League.

21. Ellen Wilkinson (1891-1947): USDAW organiser; member of CP 1920-24; Labour MP 1924-31, 1935-47; Minister of Education in the Attlee government; led Jarrow march 1936.

22. For an account of the actual course of events in the October revolution, see E.H.Carr, *The Bolshevik Revolution*, Macmillan, *1917-1923*, 1950, vol. 1, pp.105-109.

2. The Party of a New Type

1. M.Dobb in *Labour Monthly*, August 1940.

2. T.Bell, *The British Communist Party: A Short History*, Lawrence & Wishart 1937, p.83.

3. J.Degras (ed.), *The Communist International, 1919-1943: Documents*, (3 vols. 1956, 1960, 1965), Oxford University Press, under auspices of Royal Institute of International Affairs, vol. I, p.257.

4. *ibid.* p.257.

5. See R.Postgate, *The Life of George Lansbury*, Longmans Green 1951, pp.216-20.

6. See C.L.Mowat, *Britain between the Wars*, Methuen 1955, pp.125ff.

7. This method was abandoned at the Leeds congress in 1929 and a panel system adopted, i.e. delegates were presented with a list of candidates recommended by the existing executive as suitable to serve on the executive. Although this did not preclude the possibility of nominations from the floor, it was a very effective way of tightening control by the bureaucracy.

8. The 'workers' control' question was central to the controversy aroused in the Russian party by the Workers' Opposition, whose ideas, according to Kollontai, found their first, incomplete expression at the party congress in 1920.

9. The Red International of Labour Unions was established in July 1921 at the time of the Third Congress of the CI. The aim of the RILU was not to split existing unions, but to win them away from the reformist Amsterdam International Federation of Trade Unions. 'We remain inside the national trade union associations and only join the Profintern (= RILU) as organisations if we succeed in winning the majority for the principles of the RILU' (ECCI resolution, February 1922).

10. See N.Wood, *Communism and British Intellectuals*, Gollancz 1959, p.25.

11. Degras, *op.cit.* vol. 1, p.257.

12. *ibid.* p.258.

13. Lenin, quoted by L.Trotsky in *The Real Situation in Russia*, no date, p.126.

14. See Georges Sorel, *Reflections on Violence*, Allen & Unwin, 1925 (first published 1905), for a brilliant exposition of the politics of parliamentary socialism.

15. C.Rappoport, *La Revolution Mondiale*, Paris 1921, p.25. Rappoport resigned from the PCF after the show trials of the old Bolsheviks.

3. A Rope for the Labour Party

1. T.Bell, *The British Communist Party: A Short History*, Lawrence & Wishart 1937, p.67.

2. A.Hutt, *The Post-War History of the British Working Class*, Gollancz 1937, p.54.

3. Within two years J.T.Walton Newbold had resigned from the party; see *Plebs*, vol. 16, December 1924, p.483; and vol. 17, June 1925, p.247.

4. 'We decided that the British Communist Party should penetrate into the Labour Party. It did this with success. Nobody at the present time would demand that they should leave the Labour Party . . . The position in England is peculiar. There is a powerful party affiliated to the Second International. The masses in this organisation are responsive to our agitation . . . We must penetrate these masses, so as to win them over to the side of the communists.' G.Zinoviev, *Speech in Reply to Discussion of the Report on the Work of the ECCI*, Press Bureau of the Fifth Congress of the Comintern, Moscow, English ed. no date, pp.62-63.

5. G.Lansbury, *The Miracle of Fleet Street*, p.99.

6. See chapter 4 for further discussion of the Minority Movement.

7. *The Communist International; Between the Fifth and Sixth World Congresses*, CPGB, July 1928, p.122.

8. *The Eighth Congress of the CPGB*, CPGB 1927, p.44.

9. J.Degras (ed.) *The Communist International, 1919-1943: Documents* (3 vols.), OUP, vol. I (1956), p.439.

10. *ibid.* p.437.

11. The financial dependence was touched on by Piatnitsky in his report to the organisation commission at the Fifth Congress (1 July 1924), when he said: 'We appreciate very much those of our communist parties that possess a financial basis and are self-supporting'. *Les Questions d'Organisation au Ve Congrès de l'IC*, Paris 1925, p.13. The CPGB was not one of the self-supporting parties.

12. George Lansbury (1859-1940): Labour MP 1910-12, 1922-40; founder and Editor of *Daily Herald,* leader of Labour Party 1932-35.
13. David Kirkwood (1872-1955): Clyde shop steward in first world war, member of ILP, Labour MP 1922-51.
14. Robert Smillie (1857-1940): president of Scottish Miners' Federation 1894-1918 and 1921-40; founder-member of ILP.
15. James Maxton (1885-1946): imprisoned for sedition 1916, chairman ILP 1926-31, 1934-39, MP 1922-46.
16. The *Workers' Weekly* was formerly the weekly *Communist*, edited by Raymond Postgate; the change-over took place in February 1923.
17. *The Communist International*, no.8.
18. *ibid.*
19. *Report of the Eighth Congress of the CPGB*, CPGB no date, p.32.
20. *Communist Review*, November 1926.
21. *Labour Monthly*, December 1927.

4. 'All Power to the General Council'

1. J.Klugmann, *History of the Communist Party of Great Britain*, vol. 1, Lawrence & Wishart 1968, p.115.
2. The British Bureau prescribed that it should be 'independent of the British Community Party, but shall work in accord and co-operation therewith, translating into the national arena the same relations as exist between the CEC of the RILU and the CI'. (*Constitution of the Red International of Labour Unions*, no date, pp.12-13. See E.H.Carr, *The Bolshevik Revolution, 1917-1923*, 1950, 3, p.400, footnote.)
3. J.Degras (ed.), *The Communist International, 1919-1943: Documents* (3 vols.), OUP, vol. 2 (1960), p.137.
4. Tomsky: a Right Communist; ousted from his trade-union post at the Eighth Congress of the Russian unions in November 1928. He anticipated arrest, trial and execution by committing suicide in 1936, during the Zinoviev – Kamenev trial.
5. See E.H.Carr, *A History of Soviet Russia: Socialism in One Country*, vol. 3, part 1, p.585.
6. *Getting Together*, p.97.
7. A.Lozovsky, *British and Russian Workers*, National Minority Movement pamphlet no date, p.14.
8. D.Petrovski, *Das Anglo-Russische Kommittee und die Opposition in der KPSU*, Berlin 1927, p.14. A pamphlet published for the German party as ammunition against the Opposition in the Russian party.
9. cf. Carr, *op.cit.* vol. 3, part 1, p.377.
10. See Degras, *op.cit.* vol. 2, pp.264-65.
11. *International Press Correspondence*, 6 August 1925. See also

L.J.Macfarlane, *The British Communist Party: Its Origin and Development until 1929*, MacGibbon & Kee 1966, p.155.

12. For an excellent account of their miserable performance, see Christopher Farman, *The General Strike*, Panther 1974, ch.15 'The Surrender'.

13. Klugmann, *op.cit.* vol. 2 (1969), p.46, writes that this slogan 'may seem strange to later generations of militant trade unionists' and puts in a defence that he himself evidently finds unconvincing, for he concludes: 'But it can still be questioned whether this was a correct demand, whether it was correct to insist on full powers for the General Council.' Yet still later in the book we find: 'In big, bold letters the paper (i.e. *Workers' Weekly*, 8 January 1926) put forward the party's own proposals, in slogan form, the measure of *real precaution* (Klugmann's own emphasis) for the struggles ahead.' And the concluding slogan was 'All Power to the General Council' (pp.94-95).

14. P.Dutt, *The Meaning of the General Strike*, CPGB pamphlet no date, pp.17-18.

15. *ibid.* p.36.

16. Article of 22 March 1925, in J.Degras (ed.), *Soviet Documents on Foreign Policy* (3 vols. 1951, 1952, 1953), Oxford University Press under auspices of Royal Institute of International Affairs, vol. 2 (*1925-1932*), p.22.

17. L.Trotsky, *My Life*, 1930, p.450.

18. The CI after Lenin's death instructed the Chinese CP to ally with the nationalist Kuomintang, led by Chiang Kai-shek. Chiang accepted CP support till he was strong enough to act without it; then, in 1927, he turned on the CP. Between 1927 and 1930 the Chinese CP lost 30,000 killed.

19. The Trades Disputes and Trade Union Act was passed by the Baldwin Government after the defeat of the General Strike. It made illegal sympathetic strikes and strikes 'designed or calculated to coerce the government either directly or by inflicting hardship upon the community'; restricted the right of picketing, defining 'intimidation' so loosely that any effective picketing could be declared illegal; made it necessary for trade unionists to 'contract in' rather than, as formerly, 'contract out' of the political levy paid to the Labour Party (i.e. declare their willingness to pay it, not their refusal); forbade all civil servants and public employees to affiliate to the TUC. The Act was repealed by the Labour government of 1946. Laws against 'combinations' of workmen have been enacted since the thirteenth century. The most recent 'union-bashing' measure was, of course, the Industrial Relations Act.

5. Stalinisation of the CPGB

1. N.I.Bukharin: President of the CI after Zinoviev had been ousted, a direct result of the Russian inner-party conflict; author of the *Programme of the Communist International*; editor of *Pravda*; characterised by Lenin in his *Testament* as 'the favourite of the party' and the party's best theoretician; collaborated with Stalin 1923 to 1927; relieved of all his posts in 1929; expelled from the Politburo 1929; one of the accused in 1938 Moscow trial; found guilty of treason and shot.

2. The word 'bolsheviks' was dropped from the title at the Nineteenth Congress in 1952, just before Stalin's death.

3. *Fifteenth Congress of the CPSU* (*b*), Moscow, English ed. 1950, p.26.

4. *ibid.*

5. Voikov's death was also attributed to the British. 'The hand of the white guards who shot down Voikov was guided by the wire-pullers in London.' (ECCI manifesto of November 1927, in Degras, *op.cit.* vol. 2, p.409.)

6. *ibid.* p.29. K.G.Rakovsky, Ambassador in France and a member of the Trotskyist opposition, caused an uproar by signing a manifesto urging workers and soldiers to defend the Soviet Union in the event of war. Already under attack in the French press for his revolutionary attitude, this caused him to be declared *persona non grata* (cf. I.Deutscher, *The Prophet Unarmed*, OUP 1959, p.362).

7. J.Degras (ed.), *Soviet Documents on Foreign Policy*, (3 vols.), OUP, vol. 2 *1925-1932* (1952), p.236-37.

8. *ibid.* p.237.

9. *ibid.* p.237.

10. J.T.Murphy: CPGB representative on the Presidium of the ECCI, had been accorded the 'honour' of moving the Presideum resolution expelling Trotsky and Vuyovich from the ECCI on 28 September 1927.

11. *Documents of the Tenth Congress of the CPGB*, CPGB 1929, p.23.

12. *Communist Policy in Great Britain*, CPGB September 1928, pp.46-47, carry Bukharin's contribution to the discussion.

13. *ibid.* pp.41ff.

14. *ibid.* p.165.

15. *ibid.* p.172.

6. Left Turn

1. The ECCI (Executive Committee of the Communist International) was a large body on which most of the major CPs were represented.

After 1924 it met roughly once a year, and more and more took over the role of CI Congresses. After 1933 the ECCI did not meet in full session, and was replaced by the smaller Presidium.

2. *Lenin on Britain*, 1934, pp.272-73.

3. Before the Comintern was founded, the Council of People's Commissars passed the following decree of 26 December 1917:

> Taking into consideration that the Soviet Government is based on the principle of international solidarity of the proletariat and of the brotherhood of toilers of all countries; that the struggle against war and imperialism can be brought to a completely successful conclusion only if waged on an international scale, the Council of People's Commissars considers it necessary to offer assistance by all possible means to the left internationalist wing of the labour movement of all countries, regardless of whether these countries are at war with Russia, in alliance with Russia, or neutral.
>
> For this purpose the Council of People's Commissars decides to allocate two million roubles for the needs of the revolutionary international movement and to put this sum at the disposal of the foreign representatives of the Commissariat of Foreign Affairs. (Degras (ed.), *Soviet Documents on Foreign Policy* (3 vols.), OUP. vol. 1 *1917-1924* (1951), p.22.)

4. cf. Cmd. 3125, p.9.

5. One or two individuals were already moving to an oppositional position by 1929-30, though the first Trotskyist grouping in Britain did not emerge till 1932. For a history of the emergence of the Trotskyist opposition in the CPGB see Reg Groves, *The Balham Group*, Pluto Press 1974.

7. The 'Third Period'

1. L.Trotsky, *The Draft Programme of the Communist International: A Criticism of Fundamentals*, New York, 1929. See James P.Cannon, *The History of American Trotskyism*, 1944, pp.49ff, for an account of how this document was smuggled abroad.

2. *Communist Review*, January 1930.

3. *Labour Monthly*, May 1929.

4. *The World Situation and Economic Struggle: Theses of the Tenth Plenum,* CPGB no date, p.11.

5. For an assessment of the personalities of these three and an account of the behind-the-scenes parliamentary skulduggery, written from a social reformist viewpoint, see J.MacNeill Wear, *The Tragedy of Ramsay MacDonald*, 1938, chs.51-57.

6. *Central Committee Resolution*, CPGB pamphlet, January 1932.

7. The United Clothing Workers' Union under Sam Elsbury had an effective existence for only a few months; it was virtually dead when Elsbury broke with the party, although it lingered on till the next party zigzag to the right in 1935 brought its dissolution.

8. *Forward*, 9 March 1929.

9. Salomon Lozovsky (1878-1952): Russian Social-Democrat from 1901; general secretary of RILU 1921-37; shot in Stalin's last purge, subsequently rehabilitated.

10. Degras (ed.) *The Communist International, 1919-1943: Documents* (3 vols.), OUP, vol. 3 (1965), p.60.

11. *ibid.* p.62.

12. Engels, in *The British Labour Movement*, 1934, p.20 (an article in *The Labour Standard*, 4 April 1881).

13. Dimitri Manuilsky (1883-1952): Russian Social-Democrat from 1903, associate of Trotsky in exile; secretary of Executive Committee of Comintern 1929-34; later Foreign Minister of Ukraine.

14. The Independent Labour Party, founded in 1893, was one of the founding bodies of the Labour Party and remained a constituent part of it. In the late twenties it came more and more to represent the left of the Labour Party and came into growing conflict over discipline. In 1931 it ran separate candidates from the Labour Party, and in 1932 disaffiliated; its membership fell rapidly thereafter.

15. *Immediate Tasks Before the Party and the Working Class*, CPGB pamphlet 1932, p.5. Ralph Fox (*Communist Review*, April 1932, p.199) wrote of 'our ideological confusion which prevents us from seeing correctly the real nature of the ILP as the left hand of British fascism.'

16. Founded in April 1921, the NUWM had been led throughout by Wal Hannington, a talented organiser and a powerful agitator. In Scotland, Harry McShane proved equally outstanding in this field. Capable leaders were to be found among the unemployed in every large town. In its early years party control was played down, even encountering opposition and there was co-operation with the broad labour movement and even the TUC. But now Hannington himself was in trouble. He was removed from the CC in 1932. For an absorbing account of the movement, see Hannington's *Unemployed Struggles: 1919-1936*, Gollancz, 1936.

17. The Invergordon Mutiny – more accurately described as a demonstration against pay cuts bearing most harshly on the ordinary able seaman – occurred in September 1931 and was successful in forcing a review of the proposed cuts (see Fred Copeman's *Reason in Revolt*, 1948, and the pamphlet by Len Wincott, *Invergordon*, for first-hand accounts by the two leading figures).

18. A.Hutt, *The Post-War History of the British Working Class*, 1937, p.242.

8. Unity at Any Price

1. J.Degras (ed.), *Soviet Documents on Foreign Policy* (3 vols.), OUP, vol. 3 *1933-1941* (1953), p.45.

2. *ibid.* p.56. Precisely the same argument was advanced by Litvinov's successor Molotov, and those Soviet diplomats who were feeling out the German reaction to a 'normalisation of political relations' approach during the months preceding the Nazi-Soviet pact. Thus, for example, the Soviet chargé in Berlin 'strongly emphasised the possibility of a very clear distinction between the maxims of domestic policy on the one hand and orientation of foreign policy on the other hand' to Weizsucker, state secretary in the German Foreign Office. (*Nazi-Soviet Relations: 1939-41, Documents from the Archives of the German Foreign Office*, Department of State Publication 3023, 1948, p.14).

3. J.Stalin, *Leninism*, 1940, p.484.

4. *ibid.* p.484.

5. Dimitrov had become prominent through his defiant attitude at the Reichstag Fire trial in February 1934. The communist build-up of this had made his name known throughout the world; the relatively obscure Manuilsky was known only as chief spokesman for the 'third period' policy (see Ypsilon, *Pattern of World Revolution*, pp.246-53).

6. Georgi Dimitrov, *Selected Speeches and Articles*, 1951, p.119.

7. The 'New Deal' was the programme of social and economic reform introduced by President F.D.Roosevelt between 1933 and 1939 to try to overcome the effects of the depression. It consisted primarily of public works projects aimed at decreasing unemployment.

8. Dimitrov, *op.cit.* p.129.

9. *ibid.* p.124.

10. Degras, *op.cit.* vol. 3, p.375.

11. *Report of the 36th Annual Conference of the Labour Party*, 1936, p.208.

12. H.Pollitt, *The Labour Party and the Communist Party*, CPGB pamphlet 1936, p.11.

13. Fenner Brockway, *Inside the Left*, 1942, pp.266-67.

14. D.N.Pritt (1887-1972): lawyer, Labour MP 1935-40; then expelled from Labour Party; Independent Socialist MP till 1950; in post-war period president of British Rumanian Friendship Association, Society for Friendship with Bulgaria, British Peace Committee, etc.

9. The People's Front

1. The credentials and future careers of some of the participants may be noted: Lord Listowel: Labour Whip in the House of Lords; held various

offices in post-war Labour government; later Governor-General of Ghana. Robert Boothby: Tory MP 1924, then Baron. Seymour Cocks: Labour MP, member of Churchill's anti-appeasement group Focus. Sir John Maynard: Fabian, formerly member of Indian civil service and member of executive council of governor of Punjab. Mrs Cecil Chesterton: writer and correspondent for *Daily Express*. Edith Summerskill: Labour MP 1938-61, leading witchhunter of Bevanites in fifties. Maude Royden: suffragette and Anglican preacher. John Jagger: Labour MP and general president of National Union of Distributive and Allied Workers. Professor P.M.S.Blackett: physicist, during second world war adviser to British government on atomic energy. Vyvyan Adams: Tory MP who took anti-appeasement position.

2. The GPU 'took uncounted numbers of prisoners, whom they drove into the endless and empty plains of Siberia and the icy wastes of the Far North. As in no other war, however, the victors could neither admit nor reveal the full scope of hostilities; they had to pretend that they carried out a salutary transformation of rural Russia with the consent of the overwhelming majority' (I.Deutscher, *The Prophet Outcast*, 1963, p.90.)

3. Springhall was in 1943 sentenced to seven years for breaches of the Official Secrets Act. Although he had given a lifetime of devoted service to the Soviet Union, his death in Moscow rated only a few lines of bald comment in the *Daily Worker*.

4. *It Can Be Done*, Official report of Fourteenth Congress CPGB 1937, pp.224-25.

5. *ibid.* pp.271-72.

6. Spender's autobiography, *World Within World*, and his contribution to the symposium, *The God That Failed*, contain accounts of his relations with the CPGB. In regard to his attitude towards the Moscow trials, these accounts do not square with his article in the *Daily Worker*.

7. *Report of the Central Committee to the Fifteenth Party Congress*, CPGB 1938, pp.76-77.

8. *ibid.* p.117.

9. *Labour Monthly*, July 1938.

10. Claud Cockburn, who in 1935 left *The Times* for the *Daily Worker* where he wrote under the name of Frank Pitcairn, has claimed that it was he who invented this 'set': Geoffrey Dawson, Lady Astor, J.L.Garvin, and others, who allegedly dictated British policy at weekend gatherings at Cliveden.

11. The CP was particularly incensed by the Labour candidate, Reg Groves, being one of its former members, expelled for 'counter-revolutionary Trotskyism' (see Reg Groves, *The Balham Group*, Pluto Press 1974, for an account of the inner-party opposition to Stalinism). This was the first time a Labour candidate had not lost his deposit.

10. Left-Right, Right-Left

1. *The Attitude of the Proletariat to War*, CPGB pamphlet 1932, p.24.
2. *ibid.* p.22.
3. *ibid.* p.41.
4. Among the British supporters of this congress, held at Amsterdam, were such well-known personalities as Richard Aldington, Lord Berners, Rutland Boughton, W.J.Brown, Havelock Ellis, Norman Haire, Radclyffe Hall, C.E.M.Joad, P.Kapitza, Ethel Mannin, Kingsley Martin, John Middleton, Bertrand Russell, Virginia and Leonard Woolf, and Barbara Wootton. On the international committee were such names as Maxim Gorki, Henri Barbusse, Upton Sinclair, Mrs Sun Yat-sen, Romain Rolland, Theodore Dreiser, Albert Einstein, Heinrich Mann, and John Dos Passos.
5. J.Degras (ed.), *Soviet Documents on Foreign Policy* (3 vols.), OUP, vol. 3 *1933-1941* (1953), p.126.
6. *ibid.*
7. *Daily Worker*, 4 September 1939.
8. *Daily Worker*, 23 August 1939.
9. At the same time Gallacher, no longer ready to 'stick at nothing to win the war', produced another pamphlet, *The War and the Workers*, to demonstrate that he was now ready to do the opposite.
10. Degras, *op.cit.* pp.379-80.
11. *ibid.* p. 389.
12. From a typescript (unpublished) in the author's possession, *Answers of L.D.Trotsky to the questions of Sybil Vincent, representative of the London Daily Herald*, 18 March 1939.
13. *Labour Monthly*, April 1940.
14. Degras (ed.), *op.cit.* p.406.
15. *Labour Monthly*, September 1940.
16. *ibid.* May 1940.
17. *ibid.* June 1940.
18. *ibid.* September 1940.
19. Degras (ed.), *op.cit.* p.421.
20. *Report to the Eighteenth Congress of the CPSU (b)*, Moscow 1951, p.20.
21. Krishna Menon: Indian politician, St Pancras Labour councillor 1934-47; ambassador and minister in post-independence India.
22. The People Speak, National Committee, People's Convention, n.d. p.41.
23. L.Trotsky, *What Next: Vital Questions for the German Proletariat*, 1932, pp.34-35.
24. See M.R.Masani, *The Communist Party of India*, 1954, p.80.
25. H.Pollitt, *The Crimea Conference: Safeguard the Future*, CP pamphlet, March 1945, p.12.

Index

Adams, Vyvyan, 113,153n1
Allen, Clifford (Lord Allen of
Hurtwood), 114
anti-war congress, 128,154n4
Attlee, Clement, 117
Andrews, R.F. see Rothstein,
Andrew
Anglo-Russian Committee (ARC),
57,59,61,64,69,94
Anglo-Soviet Conference, 53
Arnot, R.Page, 18,134

Beer, Max, *A History of British
Socialism* (1929), 144n13
Bell, Thomas, 17,21,37-38
Bevan, Aneurin, 109
Blackett, Professor P.M.S. 113,
115-116,153n1
Blatchford, Robert, *Britain for
the British*, 143n5
Bond, Ralph, 81
Boothby, Robert, 113
Bramley, Fred, 55,57
British Bureau, 30,147n2; see also
Red International of Labour
Unions and National Minority
Movement
British Socialist Party (BSP), 9-11
Brockway, Fenner, 71,140
Bromley, John, 55
Buber-Neumann, Margarete, 136
Bukharin, Nikolai, 19,68,84,88,
149n1; ECCI British Commis-
sion, 72-77
Burns, Emile, *A Handbook of
Marxism*, 121

The Call, 11
Campbell, J.R. 50,80,123,134;
charged under Incitement to

Mutiny Act, 45; jailed, 60
Cannon, James P. 150n1
Carr, E.H. 145n22
Chamberlain, Sir Neville, 124,
126,130
Chesterton, Mrs Cecil, 113,153n1
Chiang Kai-shek, 66,71; **slaugh-
ters** Chinese communists,
148n18
Chicherin, G.V. 16
Churchill, Sir Winston, 46,124,
138-139
Clarion groups, 10
Clarion, The, 143n5
'Cliveden Set', 125
Clynes, J.R. 23
Cockburn, Claud, 153n10
Cocks, Seymour, 113
Cole, G.D.H. 119-120,144n13;
The People's Front (1937), 119;
Communist International
(Comintern, CI), 11,15,19,21,
23,43,44,131; subsidies to
party, 25; party structure, 34;
envoys to individual parties,
42; fails to convene, 81; and
revolutionary stance on war,
127-128
Communist Review, 81
Communist Party of Great
Britain (CPGB), re-organisation report (1922), 24-34; workers' control, 29; Labour Party
affiliation, 37; supports Labour
government 1924, 44; opposes
Labour Party, 1929, 81; drastic
drop in membership, 83; subsidies question, 86; inner-party
criticism, 89; ultra-leftism
brings isolation, 93-94; supports